IMMORTALITY

IMMORTALITY

A Traveler's Guide

Pir Zia Inayat Khan

Richmond, Virginia

Published by Sulūk Press

112 East Cary Street | Richmond, Virginia 23219
sulukpress.com

©2023 Omega Publications, Inc.

Editor: Cannon Labrie
Cover design and interior artwork: Hayat Nil Göksun Kılıç
Interior design: Missy Reynolds of Clothilde Designs

Printed on acid-free paper.

ISBN 978-1-941810-42-2

Names: Inayat Khan, Zia (1971–) author
Title: Immortality: A Traveler's Guide
Description: First Edition. Richmond: Sulūk Press, 2023
Identifiers: LCCN 2023931815 | ISBN 9781941810422 (paperback)
Subjects: LCSH: Sufism | Soul | BISAC: Religion/Sufi | Religion/Mysticism |
Body, Mind & Spirit/Mindfulness & Meditation

Printed and bound in the United States of America
by McNaughton & Gunn

Preface

The Soul Whence and Whither is the record of a series of lectures given by Hazrat Inayat Khan in 1923 at the Sufi Summer School in Suresnes, France. In these lectures, Hazrat traced the journey of the human soul from its primal inception to its ultimate destiny. Though still relatively little known, Hazrat's account of the soul's peregrinations is a masterpiece of mystical literature. Unlike most writings of its kind, its foundations rest on the solid ground of the author's direct spiritual perceptions, rather than on the theological speculations of preceding centuries. In this regard, *The Soul* is a book of rare significance, brimming with momentous implications.

A hundred commentaries would not suffice to exhaust the teeming meanings that radiate from the pages of *The Soul*. It is hoped that this little volume, coming a century after Hazrat's lectures were given, will be only the first among many such works of interpretation.

References and allusions to the revelations of several world scriptures can be observed throughout *The Soul*, as well as resonances with the philosophies of Plotinus, Shankaracharya, Ibn 'Arabi, and other great thinkers. Tracing these associations, however, is not the purpose of this book. Instead, the aim is to invite the reader into a personal exploration of the states of being Hazrat describes.

The passages in bold that lead off each numbered section comprise an abridged rendering of the substance of *The Soul*. Since the present book is meant as an elementary key to Hazrat's masterpiece rather than a comprehensive analysis of the whole of it, a policy of "less is more" has been adopted. Readers looking to immerse themselves in *The Soul* in its entirety are encouraged to read the recent *Centennial Edition* version or the earlier paperback version entitled *The Soul's Journey*, both of which contain the complete lectures as well as Hazrat's answers to questions posed by his listeners.[1] At the back of this book is a table showing where the paragraphs featured in this abridgement appear in the complete text as presented in these two editions.

Following each passage in bold, a segment of commentary appears in plain text. The intention of these paragraphs is to underscore the insights communicated in Hazrat's words and to gently unravel some of their nuances.

After the commentarial passages comes text in italics. Here, the reader is invited to take up a contemplation related to the theme Hazrat is articulating. Some of the contemplations take the form of exercises that can be practiced in a single sitting, while others convey orientations of a more ongoing nature. Rather than reading the book straight through, the reader is encouraged to go through it slowly, pausing to engage with

---

1. *The Inner Life*, vol. 1, *The Sufi Message of Hazrat Inayat Khan: Centennial Edition* (New Lebanon, NY: Sulūk Press, 2016) and *The Soul's Journey* (New Lebanon, NY: Omega Publications, 2016); *The Soul's Journey*, edited with a preface by Kore Salvato (New Lebanon, NY: Omega Publications, 2003).

the exercises along the way. In this way, the small book you hold in your hands may prove to be considerably expansive.

When taken to heart, Hazrat's unveilings carry the power to vastly magnify our horizons of vision and to profoundly transform our understanding of who we are. Prepare yourself, dear reader, for a tour of the sprawling inner pathways of the universe, and for an eye-opening glimpse of the meaning of it all.

·1·

Before manifestation, what existed? The essence, the truly existing, the Only Being. In what form? In no form. As what? As nothing. The only definition that words can give is: the Absolute.

Our exploration begins before the beginning. Before there was anything there was everything and nothing. The everything-and-nothing was everywhere and nowhere.

Words belong to form, but our origin lies beyond form. So words can only take us so far. The word *absolute* tries to go the distance, and nearly gets there. But it stops and turns back when it realizes it can't say the unsayable.

When a bird is singing nearby, give your attention to it. Then gently close your ears with your fingers. Listen to the silence you discover. Can you sense how the song of the bird lives silently in that soundlessness forever? Now open your ears. Can you hear how the silence generously pours itself out in the song of the bird?

Consciousness arose out of this Absolute, the consciousness of existence. There was nothing of which the Absolute could be conscious—only of its existence.

Consciousness *arose*. How do we know? Because we rise every day: Every morning we rise from sleep. We rise from inwardness to outwardness to meet the rising sun. We rub the sleep from our eyes, pull the covers off our bodies, and roll out of bed.

Before going to sleep, resolve to wake up slowly in the morning. When you wake up, wake up very slowly. Don't open your eyes right away. Don't move your body yet. Give yourself the chance to be awake, but only just awake. Let awakeness suffice. This isn't the time to look at anything, think of anything, or do anything. Just rest for a minute or two in simple, unadorned awareness. Simply be aware of being aware.

· 3 ·

Out of this consciousness of existence a feeling developed, a feeling that *I* exist. It was a development of the consciousness of existence. It is this development that formed the ego, the Logos.

You and I are different people. And yet we both refer to ourselves by the same word: "I." So does everyone in the world, and in every imaginable world. Whether I'm here or somewhere else, glum or elated, speeding along or sitting tight, I am always I. So are you, wherever you are and whatever you're doing. The I never changes; it simply watches.

At the back of your I and mine is one and the same I. By whatever name we choose to call it, this same I lives in all of us and experiences life through us all.

Close your eyes. How do you feel? Are you hungry or tired or restless? Acknowledge your mood. Then ask yourself a question: "Who is it that feels this way?" Meet the I who feels hungry or tired or restless, or however you are feeling. Recognize it as the same I who has seen, felt, and known everything you have experienced in your life.

With the feeling of the *I-ness*, the innate power of the Absolute, so to speak, pulled itself together. In other words, concentrated on one point. Thus the all-pervading radiance formed its center, the center that is the Divine Spirit, or the light.

This centered light then divided existence into two forms: the light and darkness. In fact there is no such thing as darkness, there has never been darkness; it is only more light compared with less light.

Imagine trying to play chess with all white or all black pieces. Contrast brings definition. For the single I to realize itself in many I's, time and space are needed. By means of time and space, the general becomes specific. In the loom of manifestation, a bale of wool becomes a carpet.

First there was light, but nothing to see. Then the light drew itself to a point. The point floated in emptiness. Suddenly it glimmered, glowed, flashed, and shot out rays in every direction. The universe, and we ourselves, are the tapestry woven of those beams.

Give your attention to the quality of the light as day passes into night, and again as night yields to day. In the morning, watch as the sun bursts over the horizon, lights up the sky, and sends long shadows over the earth. At midday, the sun is too bright to look at, and shadows are few. Toward sunset, long shadows return, the sun sinks down in a crimson blaze, and the sky turns from blue to black. Only then do the stars and moon appear. Notice how each phase of day and night allows a certain kind of vision. Observe how light is never completely absent.

This light and darkness formed an accommodation, a mold. And the phenomenon of light and shade, working through this mold, furthered the manifestation into a great many accommodations. Every step manifestation has taken, a variety of forms has been the result.

The universe is dappled with starlight and shadow. In this dappling, myriad creatures find niches in which to spring to life and pursue their ends. The universe is a vast home teeming with homes large and small. Every home brings forth the inhabitant perfectly suited to live, breathe, and find joy in it.

Walk through the rooms of your home. If you are thankful for the shelter these rooms give you, find a way to express that thankfulness in your mind and heart. When you next have a chance, step outside and walk around your neighborhood, greeting neighbors and passers-by along the way. Again, express thanks for the place that harbors you—its streets, its trees, its air, its light. Then think of the earth as a whole, the solar system, and the Milky Way. Give thanks for each of these havens. It is good to be home.

Out of these forms gradually came, from the mineral, the vegetable kingdom; from the vegetable, the animal kingdom; and from the animal, the human race. Thus the Divine Spirit was provided the bodies that it has needed from the time it centered itself on one point, and from there, spread its rays as various souls.

We are human because a rain cloud is a rain cloud, a cornfield is a cornfield, and a gazelle is a gazelle. We are all bound together—still things, flowing things, flowering things, walking things, thinking things—and we make each other ourselves. The bubbling up of bodies of all shapes, colors, and kinds shows the enthusiasm for every kind of experience in the spirit that lives in us.

Spend five minutes with a stone, a plant, or an animal. Feel how, just as you have your life, it has its own. Spirit loves you both, and loves to experience itself through both manifestations. Close your eyes and sense how the stone or plant or animal has found a place in your soul.

Besides the phenomenon of four elements—the air, the fire, the water, and the earth—there is one, the ether, that is the source and goal of all the elements, making them five. These elements have worked in consonance with one another and against one another, in order to bring about the results desired by the divine wisdom working behind them.

Wherever we find ourselves, we are always in the company of four friends, and a mysterious fifth. Earth always impresses with its firmness. Whatever sloshes and drips tells us it's water. Fire warms our hands and air fills our lungs.

The mysterious fifth, ether, is a consummately discreet host. It receives a constant train of guests, but is too shy to ever appear.

Dig a little hole in the ground, perhaps in sand, and bury your feet in it. "Nature rejoices in nature." Feel how the earth inside you shares a common spirit with the earth outside. Another time, sit beside a stream or pond and dip your feet in it. Feel how the water inside you shares a common spirit with the water outside. Still another time, light a candle and calmly watch the flame. Feel how the fire inside you shares a common spirit with the fire outside. Yet another time, go outside when a breeze is blowing. Refresh yourself with the freshness of the breeze. Feel how the air inside you shares a common spirit with the air outside. After each of these moments of enjoyment, pause and nod to the mysterious fifth within which earth, water, fire, and air take shape.

·8·

In humanity, the purpose of manifestation is fully accomplished, especially in such as those who have, on their return journey, become more and more conscious of their purpose by widening their outlook and by living a fuller life; those who have reached that stage of realization that is called *divinity*, in which is the fulfillment of the purpose of this whole manifestation.

All beings have their destiny and their fulfillment. Every kind of entity is a unique outpouring of the wellspring from which we have all come. This is a book for humans and about humans. Other species have their own books, or don't need books. We owe the paper and ink of this book to sprawling forests and long-slumbering fossils.

To be born as a human being is not the end of the story of the universe. It's the beginning of a story in which the source of the universe unveils itself anew.

Ask yourself, "What is a full life?" What quickenings of body, mind, and heart widen your horizons, extend your vision, and elevate your emotion? Has there been a knot in your chest? Are you ready to unravel it and breathe freely? Throughout the day, keep coming back to the thought, "I will live fully."

·9·

The Divine Spirit is known by the mystics of all ages as the sun, and therefore, in all ancient mystical symbols, the sun has been pictured as the sign of God.

The sun is that aspect of the absolute God in which God begins to manifest; and God's first step toward manifestation is God's contraction, that contraction that is seen in all living beings and in all objects. It is first contraction that takes place, and next, expansion. The former tendency is the desire of inhalation, and the latter, of exhalation.

Winter, night, sleep, inhalation, and death have something in common. Each, in its way, is a contraction. And as we well know, for every contraction there is an expansion. There is no ebb without flow, no taking away without giving back. When winter loosens its icy grip, greenery wells up in extravagant flourishes. When night exhausts itself, dawn breaks and fills the sky with its radiance. After every inhalation, an exhalation billows out. Likewise, we may be sure, there is life after death.

Close your eyes or keep them open, as you prefer. As you breathe in and out, notice how your chest and belly rise and fall. Now shift your attention to the substance of your breath.

As you inhale, see how it draws in. As you exhale, see how it flows out. While breathing gently and rhythmically, with each inhalation draw the breath deeper within, as though reaching toward a point at the center of yourself. With each exhalation, let your breath expand wider and wider, unfurling toward the horizon in every direction. At the same time, it rises up into the sky and sinks down into the ground. You could imagine your breath as a sphere that converges and intensifies as you breathe in and expands and dims as you exhale.

·10·

In plain words, manifestation is the exhalation of God; and destruction, the end of the world, is the inhalation of God. The Divine Spirit spreads itself, which we call *manifestation*, containing various names and forms; and God contracts, which humanity dreads and calls *destruction*.

The beginning and the end of the world is only God's one breath, the duration of which is numberless years. Between this one breath, myriad lives have been born, lived, and died, and have experienced this world and that world, heaven and the contrary place, all.

Endings come in many sizes—little, middling, and big. One day you and I will die. Another day, our cherished planet will crumble to dust. Yet another day, the whole universe will perish, with all its starry riches. Still, nothing is ever lost for good, and every ending spells a new beginning. The inrushing and outflowing of the divine breath goes on forever.

With eyes open or closed, watch your breath flow in and out. After a full inhalation, pause briefly. Feel the state of suspense you have been brought to. It is as if time stands still. Then let nature take its course and breathe out again. Give yourself over to the new dispensation of life and breath rolling out from within you.

·11·

There are living creatures, small germs and worms and insects, who do not live longer than a moment. And there are other beings whose life is for a hundred years, and some creatures who live longer still; and yet it is a moment, even if it were a thousand years, compared with eternity. The tendency of the mystic is to bend the head low in worship as the thought of the eternal life of God, the Only Being, comes to mind.

Time is as we regard it. To a mayfly a single day is a generous lifetime, but to a tortoise long decades are just the beginning. Our own life span will be as long or as short as the meaning we find in it.

All meaning comes from, and returns to, the One. A miraculous alchemy occurs in between, and that is what this book is about.

For a few nights in a row, every evening before going to bed ask yourself, "Was it a long day or short one?" You might find that every day has a different length. Some days speed by, others crawl along. What accounts for the difference? Are you in time, or is time in you?

·12·

The soul, which is the ray of the divine sun in one sphere, the sphere in which it does not touch any earthly being, is called *angel*. Therefore, every soul passes through the angelic plane. In other words, every soul is an angel before it touches the earthly plane. It is angels who become human beings, and those who do not become human beings remain angels. A human being, therefore, is a grown-up angel; and an angel, therefore, is a soul who never grew up.

Souls emerge from the Soul of souls in the same way that rays fan out from the sun. As many rays as the sun sends out, its light never diminishes in the slightest. The farther a ray travels earthward, the more distinct it becomes. Finally, the ray squeezes through the curtains in a dark room, and you see it as a shaft speckled with dust.

A ray poised near the corona is called an angel. It may stay in that nearly placeless place, or it may descend. If it descends, it will grow up. Or shall we say, it will grow down. It will sink a root down into the earth, and from that root rise up.

There is nothing here that wasn't there first. There may be souls without earthly bodies, but there are no bodies without souls.

Close your eyes, breathe slowly, and relax. Relax your body from head to toe. Let all tension and heaviness dissipate, so that every part of your body is at ease. Next, relax your mind. Let your thoughts soften, dissolve, and disappear like mist. If a thought lingers, not to worry. Simply pay it no heed; just let it be. Now let your feelings too melt away. Let light be the sole object of your attention. But rather than thinking about light, be light. For a little while, experience yourself as simply this: a light that has manifested from the light that is eternal. When you are ready, open your eyes again. Whatever you see in your surroundings, recognize that its essence, too, is light.

·13·

Infants, who come on earth with their angelic qualities and sometimes pass away without having experienced the life of the grown-up human, show us the same picture of the original condition of the soul. The idea that the angels are nearer to God, according to this doctrine, is right.

It is an occasion of poignant sadness when a child does not survive long on Earth. But this too is part of destiny. Every being has its own sphere of life and work, and its own specific duty in each place to which it is appointed. Those who live and work in the heavens perform a type of work there that is different to what is done down here. Each being has its way of praising, and the praises of the angels are formidable by any reckoning.

If you have a baby in your care, or if there is one in the care of someone near you, gently let your glance rest on the innocent and sweet face and form of the little child. If there isn't a baby near, look at a picture of a baby, or simply recall one with your mind's eye. Cast your mind back to the time preceding your earliest memories. You were once, like this baby, wide-eyed, guileless, and close to the source of being–do you remember? That primal nature is always in you; you only have to uncover it.

·14·

**Someone asked the Prophet why humans were greater
than the angels—humans who cause all the bloodshed
on the earth, compared with angels who always occupy
themselves in the praise of God. The answer was that the
angels knew not anything of the earth. They knew God
and so they occupied themselves with God. But humans
are greater, for when they come on earth, they have much
to occupy themselves with in the world, and still they pursue God.**

It's easy to see humans as fallen angels. The angels are our
prototypes, but we haven't stayed innocent like them. While
they glide elegantly through spheres of light, we tramp around
in a morass of mud, and often slip. And yet, it may be that a
prayer of the heart sent up from the belly of the Great Dismal
Swamp has a meaning and a power that is difficult to match
on any heavenly peak.

*Take out a sheet of paper. With a black pen, fill the top half of
the page with words, phrases, and sentences that describe the
trials, tribulations, and limitations you have faced in life. Now
put down the black pen and take up a red pen. Using the red*

pen, fill the remainder of the page with a description of your philosophy of life and your heart's highest aspirations and discoveries. Let your writing flow as a stream of consciousness.

·15·

Souls, pure of all greed and desires that the denseness of earth gives, are angels who know nothing else but happiness, for happiness is the real nature of the soul.

We are learning the difference between pleasure and joy. When a pleasure is finished, it's finished. Afterward, one might even feel emptier than before. A joy, by contrast, lives with you always. It keeps growing, and never ends. It becomes part of the great joy that is the soul's very substance.

Recall a moment of intense joy. Can you find that same joy in yourself at this moment? It isn't an event in time or space, but a place within yourself. It's the unmistakable atmosphere your soul breathes.

·16·

Humans may continue to retain the angelic quality, even in their life on the earth as human beings; and it is the angelic quality that can be traced in some souls who show innocence and simplicity in their lives, which is not necessarily foolishness. It only shows the delicacy of a flower in a personality, together with fragrance.

Good and simple people are a living proof of heaven. It is as if they always have one foot in a realm of hidden glory. They are here and there at once. Because of this, they are able to bring heaven closer to us. Though often dismissed as know-nothings, in reality they are pillars of truth.

Think of a person whose nature is simple and kind. Call the blessings of heaven down on that person. You are only acknowledging what is already true. That person is blessed.

·17·

The picture of the angels, as we read in the scriptures, sitting upon the clouds and playing on harps, is but an expression of a mystic secret. Playing the harp is vibrating harmoniously. And sitting on the clouds only means that the angels are above all clouds.

Music is the speech of the angels. Their messages are songs that waft between the stars. The instruments they play are their own light-bodies.

We only hear the songs of the angels when the clouds of doubt and fear that vex our world part momentarily and let in the light of the higher altitudes.

At the time of going to sleep, put aside all of your worries. You can worry, and make plans again, later. For now, let go of every cause of concern. Whatever will be, will be. Now, with an easy mind and a restful heart, listen to the silence. Can you hear a quiet strain of music? If you can't, keep listening. Keep listening night after night until you hear it. When you do hear it, listen as though with your heart's ear. No need to try to capture its notes. Just let it lead you where it will, like a river wending its course to the sea.

·18·

The souls in the angelic sphere have all goodness, and this proves that goodness is natural; and what is contrary to our nature, we call it *badness*. The souls in the angelic sphere are innocent. This also shows that innocence is the natural condition of the soul, and the lack of innocence is a foreign element that the soul acquires after coming on earth.

Goodness is that which has always been in us. Whatever is fundamental to your life is by definition good. Whatever cuts you off from that foundation is . . . a problem. A problem is, of course, something to be solved. The solution might well unveil a deeper knowledge of the goodness of the good. One is prone to take something for granted until it slips out of one's hands. There is a special satisfaction in recovering a possession thought to be irretrievably lost.

Think of someone you know who has done something wrong and feels ashamed. In your mind, distinguish the misdeed from the soul of the person. Even if the person has misbehaved, or has developed bad habits, this person is not essentially bad. Deep down underneath the static, a luminous soul is still there. For a moment, imagine that you could stand before that soul as a mirror and reflect back to it the light that the One has entrusted to it forever.

·19·

Souls on the earth have something of the angelic quality, therefore they readily respond and are attracted, without resistance, to the innocence, happiness, and goodness of another person. If they knew that it is because this is the original quality of their soul, they would develop the same in their own being.

Everything is drawn to its like: the forgetful to the forgetful, the sincere to the sincere, the soulful to the soulful. If we are awake enough, a person overflowing with soul-power can remind us of what lives in our own soul, jolting us with a strange wave of nostalgia and ecstasy.

Think of someone who inspires you and puts you in touch with your soul. The resonance you feel makes you companions on the path of truth. Take a moment to notice the qualities this person embodies, and how the same qualities within you are seeking an ever-fuller place in your life.

·20·

Seeking after goodness, innocence, and happiness helps the angelic qualities to develop in a soul. Spirituality, therefore, is the development of the angelic quality; and love of spirituality is the longing for the angelic spheres. It is homesickness.

Heaven is our ancestral home. Not a faraway paradise, but the true home that has always been right here. Even if we have left it, it hasn't left us. Crawl under the fence of pride, climb over the wall of shame, and you have arrived. The angels are our long-lost family, eager to welcome us back.

Close your eyes and relax. Let your breath become slow, deep, and fine. Give all of your attention to the breath as it goes out. Over eleven exhalations, silently repeat the word "home." Then shift your attention to the breath as it flows in. Listen to the news from home that these inhalations bring you, reminding you of the place to which you will always belong.

·21·

Does death frighten spiritual beings? No, death for the spiritual soul is only a gate, a door, through which it enters into that sphere that every soul has known to be its home. Souls who become conscious of the angelic sphere, even to the smallest degree, hear the calling of that sphere; and if they have any discomfort in this world, it is that home-sickness that the call of the angelic sphere gives.

Death might seem like a journey into the unknown. In fact, it's a return to the home we have always known. It isn't an exile so much as a reunion. Those who learn to walk in and out through the doors of the senses lose all fear of death. When death comes, they know where they are going.

For a day or longer, whenever you cross a threshold make it a point to step across with your right foot first. Keep this up whether entering or leaving the house, and even when going from room to room indoors. See how you become conscious of moving between spaces in a new way. Let your step be intentional and optimistic, so that you enter each new space purposefully. Notice that there are, likewise, spaces within the world of the mind. Pay attention when moving from one to another.

·22·

The soul may be likened to a ray of the sun; so the souls of angels, not being adorned with physical garb, are lights, are flames themselves. The scriptures, therefore, say the angels are made of light. In short, all souls are made of that essence that is the essence of the whole manifestation.

The essence of everything is a blazing light. When you look deeply into someone's eyes, that light is what you see. It's the living flame that peers through their eyes and listens through their ears. It's their angelhood. Your own angelhood looks out through your eyes. The substance of both lights belongs to the white-hot core of creation.

Put something on a table in front of you. It could be a piece of fruit, or a car key. Gaze at it calmly. But now, instead of giving your attention to the object, give your attention to your glance. Notice how it seemingly comes out of nowhere. Through the interlaced instruments of your eyes, optic nerves, and brain it beams out from a light that has no particular location in space. Sense in that luminous space your angelic counterpart.

·23·

The soul going toward manifestation, which is still in the angelic spheres, is free from all differences and distinctions which are the conditions of the soul's life on earth. Are angels male and female? This question can be answered that the dual aspect starts even from the angelic spheres. God alone is above this aspect, but in all other conditions and aspects of life, this aspect is to be seen, though this difference is more distinct on the earth plane. In the angelic plane it is not distinguishable.

Differences are fewer in the inner planes as compared with the outer world, where human attention generally resides. Those who begin to see everything reflected in its opposite see deeper into life and enter the inner dimensions of existence.

Bring your attention back to the light that looks out through your eyes. If you are male, is it male? If you are female, is it female? Do you sense a particular gender when you cause yourself to be aware of it? Or do you sense a state of being that is somehow beyond the gender categories familiar to our ordinary identity?

·24·

And now there is another question: Are the angels in touch with people on earth? And the answer is that their life does not necessitate any communication with human life on earth, except some who are destined to perform a certain duty on the earth.

Numerous angels live happily in the netherworld and have no need to venture further afield. Others descend to become jinn, stones, plants, and various kinds of animals, including human beings. Still others remain as angels, but are dispatched from time to time to fulfill specific duties for the benefit of beings on other planes.

Close your eyes. Think of a forest near your home. How many birds and squirrels live in its trees? How many worms and microscopic insects live in its soil? You will probably never see more than a small number of them. Think of another forest, and another, and a lake, and an ocean, and all of the teeming habitats of our world. How many beings live out their lives in these many zones of earth and water—beings we will never know, but with whom we are nonetheless somehow related?

Think likewise of the myriad invisible beings we call angels. Some you may meet; many you will not. We each move in our own orbit, yet we are all part of the same encompassing whole.

·25·

In the exceptional lives of the prophets, what happens is that they rise above all the planes that keep a person removed from the angelic plane; and by doing so, they are able to touch that angelic plane. And being charged with the ever-glowing fire of inspiration from the angelic spheres where they come in touch with angels, they descend to the plane of the earth. The soul of the prophet, therefore, is a link between heaven and the earth; it is a medium by which God's message can be received.

Revelations are not the product of human contrivance. Revelation comes when the veil between worlds is parted. Spirit and body recognize each other anew, and angelic vision becomes human speech.

Think of a prophet or prophetess who has brought a message of divine remembrance to the world. It is difficult to know what the prophet or prophetess might have looked like in life. Rather than trying to visualize this great figure, try to feel the flame of truth burning in their heart. Let the warmth and light of that flame spread to your heart.

·26·

Then there are some pious souls who have the experience in their lives of having been warned or helped by an angel. It is such souls who have kept a thread unbroken, which they brought with them from the angelic world. They may be conscious of it or not, but there is a telegraphic wire which connects their souls with the souls of the angels, and they are conscious of having had contact with the angels.

Contact with angels often happens in times of special need. When all is going well, the angels may seem distant and aloof. Then suddenly there is a crisis, and in the darkest hour of that Dark Night an angel appears garbed in light. Is it because our vulnerability elicits the angels' compassion? Or is it that the rawness we feel at such moments exposes our senses to subtler spheres?

Close your eyes. Eleven times, breathe out the silent question to heaven, "Have you helped me?" Then be inwardly silent and listen for the answer. Listen closely with each inhalation. Now, eleven times, breathe out the question, "Will you help me?" Again, listen for the answer. Sense that there is a thread connecting you to the angelic sphere. By means of this thread, you may send a prayer into the highest reaches of existence at any time, and a response is sure to come, whether in a form recognizable or mysterious.

·27·

When many cannot experience something that is rare, they think the person who experiences it has gone crazy. Therefore, it is the law of the mystics to see all things, to experience all things either of the earth or of heaven, and yet say little; for the souls incapable of understanding the possibility of their reach will only mock at them.

If you converse with angels, or even simply believe them, it may be best to be a bit discreet about it. It's up to you, of course. But you need not feel obliged to convince anyone of anything. Your discoveries are your own. Everyone will discover the angels sooner or later, whether in this life or the next.

Think of something you have never told anyone. Maybe the day will come when you will tell it to someone, if the moment is right. Meanwhile, it lives in a hidden place inside you. Your secret is no less unreal for being unspoken. It's in the keeping of the One.

·28·

There is another aspect of the contact with the angels, and that is at the time of death. Many have seen in their lives the angels of death, but at the time when death's call comes, some have seen them in a human form. Some have not seen them but heard them speak. The reason is that there are some souls who have already departed from the earth plane, though the breath is still there, connecting the soul with the body; and such souls experience, while still on earth, the angelic sphere at the time of their death. They see angels garbed in the form of their own imagination and hear their words in their own language. The reason is that it is necessary for a person who has lived on the earthly plane to clothe a being on the higher planes in earthly garments, and to interpret immediately the language of the higher sphere in one's own words.

Angels often appear during near-death experiences. When they appear in a tangible form and speak in a language the hearer understands, it's because the encounter is taking place in the world of immaterial images, where spirits are corporealized and bodies are spiritualized. The angel's celestial form has no fixed contours, but within the realm of images the angel takes on a recognizable aspect for the purpose of communicating with a human mind.

Close your eyes and recall the generous, numinous and inspiring figures you have seen in dreams and visions. Perhaps one being comes especially to mind. Has this being appeared to you more than once? Can you sense behind its form, or succession of forms, an underlying angelic light?

·29·

The angel Gabriel spoke to Moses in the Hebrew language and to Muhammad in Arabic. One would ask, what was the language of Gabriel, Arabic or Hebrew? Neither Arabic nor Hebrew was the language of Gabriel. Gabriel's language was the language of the soul, and the soul knows the language of the soul. When the soul interprets what it hears, even to itself, then it garbs the words in its own language.

To be received by human ears, the divine speech that pours out of eternity must be interpreted in human language. In the angelic plane, revelation manifests in the language of the soul. The prophet's soul then translates it into the language of the earthly time and place to which the prophet belongs. Since words in human language can be taken many ways, and are sometimes changed or forgotten, believers often find themselves at odds. Behind the words, however, is a current of spirit that gives life to the world. This is the soul of scripture.

When listening to someone speak, shift your attention from their words to the tone of their voice. Then, after a little while, turn your attention to the speaker's breath, the invisible substance from which their words are molded. Finally, give your attention to the inner spirit or consciousness that moves the speaker's breath.

·30·

There is a phrase known to many: *the guardian angel*. This angel's protection comes to some souls on earth, such souls who are walking on the earth and yet are linked in some way or the other to the heavenly spheres. Often one sees an innocent child being saved from several accidents, and often a person is warned to save a child at the moment when the child is in danger. This guardian angel also appears in the same form as angels sent to people on different duties.

A materialist recognizes only physical causes and effects. But there are realities beyond the physical plane. The truth of the matter is more like three-dimensional chess. A rook from above sometimes descends down and a pawn from below sometimes steps up a level. It is only fair to acknowledge the help and kindness we receive from invisible helpers in addition to the help we receive from visible well-wishers.

Think of the many ways your friends have helped you in the course of your life. Pause to offer a silent thought of gratitude. Now think of the ways in which you have been helped in a manner you can hardly understand. Think of the intuitions that have reached you as if on a breeze, sent by a mysterious protector. Again, pause to offer a silent thought of gratitude.

·31·

There are recording angels, who take a record of one's good actions and of bad actions. But the most interesting thing is that those who keep the record of good actions do not keep the record of bad actions; those who keep the record of bad actions are other angels.

There is no person living on earth of whom all say good things and no one says bad things. So there is no person living about whom all say bad things and no one says any good. And the most interesting part, for a keen observer of life, is how each tries to prove their argument to be correct.

We all have both good and bad in our character. Where one ends and the other begins isn't always clear. Someone who is consistently pious and beyond reproach runs the risk of becoming self-satisfied and pompous. At the same time, someone who has made many mistakes might prove, in the long run, endearingly humble and sincere. Is it any wonder that the recording angels tend to argue between themselves?

Think of someone you know. In your mind, enumerate the things that bother you about that person. Now set all of that aside and make note of the things that you appreciate about

the person. Notice how on some days you are more prone to see-
ing the positive qualities and on other days the contrary ones.
You might further notice how the two kinds of qualities are to
some extent intertwined. What is more, the whole complex of
traits that makes up the person is dynamic rather than static,
and so it is subject to continual change. Now make yourself the
subject of your contemplation, and go through the same steps.

·32·

There is a story in the Bible that Jacob wrestled with the angel all night, and in the end, before the breaking of the morn, Jacob won. And the angel asked his name and blessed him. The interpretation of this is that the illuminated souls of the angels, coming in contact with the earthly beings, are in conflict. And that conflict ends when a person has given up the earthly point of view and has adopted the heavenly point of view; then there is no more conflict, but a blessing.

An encounter with an angel isn't always easy. The angel's consciousness is too vast, too transgalactic, to easily sync with a mentality ensconced in four walls. A duel of conflicting visions tends to follow. In cases of this kind, the coup de grâce the angel at last delivers is only a blow to the other's illusions. Both combatants win.

Watch an ant walk along the ground. It's likely following a scent trail. Though you are looming over it, it probably isn't particularly aware of you. It's living in its own little world. Consider how you, too, are living in your own little world. Immense presences are swirling around us, but we tend to pay them little heed. Take a moment to acknowledge the vast universe around you. Acknowledge that you see only as much as you are shown, and prepare yourself to be shown more when it is meant to be revealed to you. Cultivate an attitude of open-mindedness, curiosity, and a readiness to be stretched in your perceptions and perspectives.

·33·

The angels who are related to human beings are human souls, now in the angelic world, who keep a connection with human beings because of their wish. And now that they have gone back from earthly regions to the angelic world, they still keep in touch with the earth, either being on a certain duty or because of their own pleasure.

When some people die and leave the physical world, they make their way through the worlds beyond and never really look back. Others remain attached to the physical world and grasp at it in various ways, sometimes with great frustration. Still others are free from grasping attachment, but nonetheless feel a special affection for the people of the physical world and stay connected with them and offer their help.

Close your eyes and think of someone you love who has left this world. Take a few moments to discern that person's living presence within yourself. In the course of eleven exhalations, as a silent message, send the person's soul the thought of your goodwill and esteem. Then, as you inhale, watch and see if there is any inward intimation of the soul returning your greeting.

·34·

The angelic spheres, the highest heavens, are the spheres of light; and that current of power, which runs through the divine sun, causes rays to spread, each ray being an angel or a soul. It is this divine current that, really speaking, is breath or the ego. Breath is the ego, and ego is the breath. When the breath has left the body, the ego has gone. The nature of this current, which spreads as a ray and which is a life-current, is to collect and to create. It collects the atoms of the sphere in which it is running, and it creates out of itself all that it can create. Therefore, in the angelic sphere, which is the sphere of radiance, the soul collects the atoms of radiance.

The whole of creation is the exhalation of the One. That vast-sweeping deluge gives rise to innumerable currents, some great and some small. Each current takes on the nature of the planes through which it passes. Every current must first pass through the angelic realm, where it is enveloped in a body of immaterial light. Currents that flow further assume bodies of thought and matter. It is the breath that attracts, organizes, and eventually relinquishes the substances that give ever more definite form to the self as it manifests itself successively from plane to plane.

Close your eyes and let your breath become deep, slow, and fine. As you inhale, feel as though you are slowly moving backward in space. Midway into your inhalation, assume the form of your own image divested of matter. At the culmination of your inhalation, further behind your physical form, cease to identify with your image and experience yourself as a formless light made of pure awareness. For a brief moment, pause in that experience. As you exhale, return from formlessness to form, and then from form to materiality. Sense how your breath serves as a link between all three conditions of your being. Relax and notice your state.

·35·

One may ask, "If the souls who have settled in the angelic world are angels, then what makes them come to the earth? How can they experience life on the earth?" The answer is that it is not the angels who have settled who come to the earth.

Some angels are sedentary and others are nomads. The sedentary ones are not unmindful of the attraction of the horizon, but they lack a strong enough motivation to uproot themselves. They remain in the celestial spheres and fulfill their life's purpose there.

The nomads are discontent to remain where they are. A strange wanderlust compels them to seek the frontier. Form and matter are mystical states they long to know. And so they set out. We, and every other material being, are among their number. We are all migrants from the invisible world.

Look for a stone that draws your attention. Take it in your hands and hold it. Observe its color and feel its heft and texture. Roll it from palm to palm a few times. Now close your eyes. Recall, if only vaguely, the time before you had hands with which to touch something. Recognize how your soul has taken a physical body in order to have a certain kind of experience. You are having that experience now. It is good. And it is not the end.

·36·

The question very often arises, if an angel comes from above, does it descend outwardly before a person or within a person, in the heart? This question may be answered that the lift for the soul is situated within, not without, which brings the soul down to earth and takes it back toward heaven. That lift is the breath. The soul comes with the breath to earth, and with the same it returns.

Those among human beings who are not even aware of their own breath, how can they know who came within and who went away? Many seem wide awake to the life without but asleep within. And though the chamber of the heart is continually visited by the hosts of heaven, they do not know their heart, they are not there.

Outer life is so engrossing it's easy to lose sight of the life within. We see what is before us, but we rarely see our own state. To observe one's breath is to begin to turn inward. The deeper one goes, the more one discovers. Just as trillions of little organisms live in our bodies, myriad invisible beings inhabit our spirits.

Resolve to acquaint yourself with your breath closely. In the morning, take twenty conscious breaths. Throughout the day, as often as possible, bring your awareness back to your breath. At the end of the day, before going to sleep, return to this awareness. Day by day, explore increasingly subtle layers within your breath.

·37·

And there is a story that tells how frightened the soul was when it was commanded to enter the body of clay. It was most unwilling, not from pride but from fear. The soul whose nature is freedom, whose dwelling is the heavens, whose comfort is to be free to dwell in all the spheres of existence—for that soul, to go and sit in a house made of clay was most horrifying. Then God asked the angels to play and sing, and the ecstasy that was produced in the soul by hearing the singing made it enter into that body of clay, where it was captive to death.

Angels are of vast proportions and live lives of long duration. What could induce an angel to enter a mortal coil and lead a hidebound life? There is an ancient music in matter, the music of the spheres. The journey of the soul is the pursuit of ever-unfolding, cosmically spiraling harmonic themes. From the heights of heaven to the depths of the earth, the soul is led constantly onward in its quest for beauty.

Put on a favorite piece of music, close your eyes, and listen attentively. There is something sublime in the arrangement of the notes, something that makes your spirit stir. When the music finishes, stay in the silence and observe the rhythm of your breath. When your breath's rhythm becomes tangible, turn your attention to the rhythm of your heart. When your heart's rhythm becomes palpable, search the interior spaces of your body, listening for signs of the subtle vibrations pulsing in them. Apprehend your body as a symphony of interwoven rhythms and tones.

·38·

**The soul that has passed through the angelic plane comes
into the plane of the jinn. It is the plane of the mind, and
this plane may be called the *spiritual plane*, for it is mind
and soul that make spirit. The souls who halt in this plane,
being attracted to the beauty of this plane, settle here.
Also the souls who have no more power to go farther into
outer manifestation become the inhabitants of this plane.**

Mind bridges the gap between consciousness and matter.
Consciousness is at first abstract and amorphous. To reach
the physical sphere, the witnessing faculty of the soul must
familiarize itself with images. When the soul incarnates on
Earth, imagery takes on the full weight of matter. In the middle world, however, images as yet float weightlessly, as in a
dream. The images of that world are far more vivid, however,
than our ordinary visions of the night. Our quotidian dreams
are the shadows of the scenes of that world.

*Place an object in front of you on the table. Gaze on it for a
while, taking its form into your mind. When you are ready,
close your eyes but continue to visualize the object exactly
as you saw it with open eyes. If the image disappears, begin*

again. With practice, you will likely find that you can hold the image in your mind for increasing lengths of time. In daily life, notice how everything has an image that you can experience internally.

·39·

The jinn is an entity with mind, but not such a mind as that of humans; but a mind more pure, more clear, which is illuminated by the light of intelligence. The mind of the jinn is deeper in perception and in conception because it is empty, not filled up with thoughts and imaginations as that of humans. It is the mind of the jinn that may be called *the empty cup*—a cup into which knowledge can be poured out, in which there is an accommodation. It is for this reason that the teachers on the spiritual path appreciate the jinn quality in the minds of their pupils, in which they find accommodation for knowledge.

The jinn mind lies halfway between angelic and human consciousness. Not as formless as the mind of an angel, it is still more diaphanous and supple than a human mind. That is because it is less burdened by preconceived notions and biases. The phrase *open-minded* well expresses the character of the jinn mind. Curious, malleable, and capacious, the mind of the jinn surveys the world of images with a noble freedom and lightness of touch.

There are many subjects on which people have contrasting opinions. We are all attached to our views and firmly believe we are right and others are wrong. The worry is that to backtrack on a judgment would be to abandon a portion of one's very selfhood. For that to be true, however, our self would have to consist of a heap of notions and attitudes. Deep down, we recognize our I-ness to be something far less random and contingent.

Think of an opinion you hold that differs from the perspective of some of the people around you. As an exercise, try suspending that opinion, which is to say, temporarily putting it aside like a garment you have taken off. Spend the day thinking and acting as if you hold the contrary point of view. Take this other side of the argument seriously, and mentally inhabit its assumptions. At the end of the day, if you wish, resume your former opinion. But resolve to keep an open mind toward those who think differently.

·40·

Subjects such as poetry, music, art, inventive science, philosophy and morals are akin to the nature of the jinn. The artist, therefore, and the poet, the musician and the philosopher, show in their gift the jinn heritage, which proves them, through life, to be geniuses.

Jinns are beings of knowledge, whose hunger is for knowledge; whose joy is in learning, in understanding; and whose work is inspiring and bringing joy and light to others. In every kind of knowledge that exists, the most favorite knowledge to a jinn is the knowledge of truth, in which is the fulfillment of its life's purpose.

Meditation means witnessing the simple, clear light of awareness. It's an angelic act. Contemplation is different. Contemplation means witnessing the qualities of being in their many unfurlings, flowerings, and cross-pollinations. Contemplation is a jinnic act.

The jinns take pleasure in knowledge in all of its forms. Their enthusiasm for discovery and creativity knows no bounds. For a jinnic mind, science and art are two sides of the same coin, both equally worthy of lifelong pursuit.

Science, art, and all of the ways of the imagination do not begin among us here in the physical world. They begin among the jinns in the world of images. Everything that is built here has its template there.

Life is a continual process of learning. Our contemplative education is either active and intentional or passive and accidental. If it's active, naturally the learning curve is more rapid, expansive, and interesting. Ask yourself: "What are the living questions I am pursuing? What are the materials I have with which to work? What constellation of cognitive discoveries is taking shape in my mind and heart? How can I quicken the furtherance of these epiphanies?"

·41·

The questions of what the jinns are like and what they look like, I will answer in the same way as I have in explaining the forms of angels. Things are not always as they are, but also as we see them. Humans always picture the beings they imagine and cannot see with their physical eyes, as something like themselves. Or human imagination may gather different forms, for instance, wings from the birds, and horns, and paws from tigers; a person puts them all together and makes a new form. It is beyond possibility to explain exactly how a jinn looks, and yet there is no existing being who lives without form.

Everything that wears a body equally possesses a soul and a mind—even if it is a mind very different from our own. All things in the physical world therefore have their origins, and still-living counterparts, in the angelic and jinnic worlds. A palm tree's jinnic body approaches its vegetal form, just as a fox's jinnic body anticipates its animal form, and your jinnic body prefigures your human form. The bodies of the jinn world, however, are like gossamer as compared to the dense stuff of material physiques.

Pay attention to your form in your dreams. Before going to sleep, say to yourself, let me notice myself in my dreams tonight. You might, additionally, wake up before you usually wake up in the morning, remind yourself to observe yourself, and go back to sleep. Develop a familiarity with your dream body. But recognize that this is still only a pale reflection of your jinnic form.

·42·

The world of jinns is the world of minds, yet the minds of jinns are not so developed as the minds of humans. The reason is that the experience of life on the earth completes the making of the mind. In the jinn world, the mind is only a design, an outline, a design that is not yet embroidered.

The world of the jinns is like an architectural studio. Blueprints and drafting tools are strewn over tables, and fiberglass models of all kinds abound, ranging from the simplest designs to the most extravagant flights of fantasy. All of these structures remain prototypes; nothing has yet been translated into concrete, brick, wood, and plaster.

Recognize how everything you have built in your life has begun as a creation within your mind. What do you plan to build next? Have you designed it first as a carefully and lovingly crafted construct of inner vision?

·43·

To the questions, what is the occupation of jinns? and what does the world of jinns look like? one may give a thousand explanations, but nothing will explain it fully. For instance, if a person would ask me what China looks like, I would say, "It is most wonderful, most interesting." But if they ask, "What is wonderful and interesting?" I would say, "Go and take a trip to China in order to see it fully."

How is one to make a trip to the Orient of the jinns? There are two routes: one vertical and the other horizontal. The vertical road is taken by closing your eyes. You efface the physical world and step into the imaginative world that precipitates around you as you wander through it. Its scenes are not entirely unfamiliar, but nonetheless contain surprises. And yet even what is surprising in the world of images somehow rings true.

The horizontal road extends straight through the physical world in which your body is embedded. To follow this route, you have to see not only the surfaces of the things that are in front of you but also their spirits. This happens when you convince yourself, without a shred of doubt, that everything has a jinnic and angelic double. The jin in you meets the jinn in whatever you are looking at.

Think of someone you dearly love who is geographically far from you. Do more than think of the person, see the person clearly with your mind's eye. See not only the person's face, but also their expression. See not only their shape, but also their posture and gestures. It doesn't matter where a person is, or even if the person still exists in the physical world. You can always approach this person through your faculty of imagination. The more you exercise this faculty, the more vivid will be its perceptions and the more tangibly the person of whom you're thinking will be able to respond to you through the image that you have of them.

We have not sufficient words to explain what a jinn is like or what the world of the jinn is. But what little can be said about it is that it is a world of music, a world of art, of poetry; a world of intelligence, cheerfulness, and joy; a world of thought, imagination, and sentiment; a world that a poet would approve of, and a musician would crave to experience.

Imagination, creativity, and beauty are the lifeblood of human flourishing. A realm in which these fountains are absent quickly parches and turns to dust. Artists, storytellers, poets, and musicians are emissaries of the world of images. Should our world ever be cut off from that world, it would soon wither and die. Every child is born to be an artist in some fashion.

Recognize your need for beauty. Count the ways in which you are quenching that need. Is there a deeper thirst? Then search out deeper wells. Pursue beauty into its most sacred and sublime recesses.

·45·

The life of the jinn is the ideal life for a thinker to be in, a life that is free from all illnesses, pure from all the bitterness of human nature, free to move about without any hindrance through space, and most joyful. There the sun of intelligence shines, the trouble of birth and death is not so severe, and life not so short as on the earth. If there is any paradise, it is the world of jinns.

The jinn live within the atmosphere of their own thoughts, and in this way surround themselves with the furnishings of paradise. Here on earth, we are subject to hard realities beyond our control. Nonetheless, the attitude we cultivate has an undeniable bearing on how we experience the world. We can enhance the meaningfulness of our various encounters by leaning into them with vision and élan.

Envision your mind as a transparent sphere that extends into the universe around you. When you see further, it expands; when you focus your gaze, it contracts. This sphere brings to light whatever it encompasses. But it also does more: it colors and even reimagines what it contains. Experiment with both properties of mind. First, extend your gaze as objectively as possible, taking in, as simply as possible, the raw data around you. Then, be conscious of the creative aspect of your gaze. See the world around you as you choose to see. As you do so, make it part of you and make yourself part of it.

·46·

The soul that goes as far as the sphere of the jinn, as a current coming from the heavens, functions in a body of the jinn world. The question is, but a soul which comes from the heavens, from the world of angels, does it come to the jinn world without a body? The answer is no. It comes with a body, an angelic body; yet it becomes necessary for the soul coming with the angelic body into the jinn world, to be adorned with a body of that particular world in order to stand the weather of that plane. The animals which live in cold countries have a different skin from those that live in tropical countries. That is the condition for going into any other sphere.

Just as caterpillars must turn into butterflies to fulfill their further destinies, an angelic body must become a jinnic body if the angel is to take up residence in the world of images. This transformation consists of a refashioning and hardening of the angel's hitherto celestial substance. If the angel-turned-jinn later resolves to become a human, an additional degree of coagulation will be required.

Give your attention water in its many transformations. See how it falls from the sky as rain, then rises up again as mist. Watch dew harden into frost and ice melt into brisk-flowing freshets. Recognize yourself as being of the nature of ice, water, and vapor all at once, like a melting, steaming glacier.

·47·

The souls who are passing through the jinn sphere toward the physical plane, and who do not stop in the jinn plane, meet with the travelers on their journey back home. They learn from them a great many things. There is a give-and-take, there is buying and selling, there is learning and teaching; but who teaches the most? The one with more experience, the one who is going back home. This gives the map of the journey to the soul traveling toward manifestation. It is from that map that the traveling soul strikes its path, rightly or wrongly.

It is therefore that every child born on earth, besides what it has inherited from its parents and ancestors, possesses a power and knowledge quite peculiar to itself, different from what its parents or ancestors possessed. Yet it knows not where it received this, nor who gave it that knowledge; but the child shows, from the beginning of its life on earth, signs of having known things that have never been taught to it.

Angels who are drawn to migrate to the world of images are often piqued by the intriguing reports they hear from souls newly returning from there. Likewise, when humans leave their physical bodies and reenter the jinnic world, they bring news from the frontier that tends to inspire footloose jinns to pack their bags and go West.

The concerns and enthusiasms of the ascending human soul have a way of rubbing off on the descending jinn, and it isn't uncommon for the jinn to adopt some of the mannerisms of the seasoned traveler that has so keenly captivated it. The human soul, in turn, benefits from having found a local guide in the world of images. It isn't only on the physical plane that friends prove mutually influential.

Think of the ways that friends and acquaintances have influenced various aspects of your personality, including the style of clothes you wear, the accent with which you speak, and the shows you watch and books you read. Are you aware of the reverse: the ways in which you have influenced others around you? Can you conceive that the social imprinting that you carry may have actually begun before you were born? Psychologists posit the existence of an inner child. Can you sense, deep within you, an inner jinn and inner angel? Can you recall, however dimly, the teachers and friends these differing personifications of yourself have known?

·48·

One soul is more impressionable than another soul. One soul is perhaps more impressed by the angelic plane, and that impression has remained deeper in that soul throughout the whole journey. There is another soul who is more impressed by the jinn world, and that impression lasts with that soul all through the journey. There is another soul who has not gotten that impression from the angelic world or from the jinn world. That soul does not know either of heaven or of the jinn plane; what it knows is from the earth, and it is only interested in the things of the earth.

People belong to three basic tribes. Some are preoccupied with their body, others with their mind, and still others with their soul. Gnostics called them hylics, psychics, and pneumatics. Each orientation has its wisdom provided it is adeptly pursued. There is a yoga of the body, a yoga of the mind, and a yoga of the soul. The most well-rounded personality shows all three strengths.

Consider how body, mind, and soul each deserve their due. Perhaps you have a greater inclination toward one or another;

that is normal. But what do the other parts of yourself need to more fully come alive in the light of spirit? How do your daily activities reflect your priorities? Do you provide your body with exercise? Do you give your mind time to study and reflect? Do you offer your soul the silence it needs to remember itself and its source?

· 49 ·

Humans are as they thinketh,[1] and what is it that humans think? They think of that in which they are most interested. And what they are most interested in, that, they themselves are. Do we not see in our life on earth some people, deeply impressed with a certain personality, ideal, thought, or feeling, having become the same in time? If that is true, what is a human being? One is one's impression. The soul, impressed deeply in the jinn world by some personality coming back from the earth, an impression deeply engraved upon that soul that the soul can never throw away, certainly becomes itself that personality with which it was impressed.

Here is the real basis of the theory of reincarnation. Souls impress each other in the world of images. As a result, descending souls bring back to the physical world talents and memories borrowed from ascending souls freshly returned from the earth.

Einstein has students among the jinn as well as among us here. A "born genius" is not necessarily untutored.

---

1. Proverbs 23:7.

If you look something up on Google you might start getting ads about it. The more you give your attention to something, the more you are likely to be drawn into it. The initial impression might have been accidental, but before long you might find yourself hooked. Consider the ways in which impressions have shaped your mind, both consciously and unconsciously. Ultimately, it's your choice which impressions to entertain and which to discard.

At the end of the day, review the various influences you have been exposed to. Pause to consider each one, and ask yourself, "Do I wish to give my time, attention, and care to this? Is it genuinely beneficial to me and to others?" If it is, consciously choose to cultivate it. If it isn't, let it go.

·50·

Life, from beginning to end, is a mystery. The deeper one dives in order to investigate the truth, the more difficulty one finds in distinguishing what is called _personality_. But it is not the aim of the wise to distinguish personality; their wisdom is in the understanding of the secret of personality, its composition and its decomposition which resolves, in the end, in the one personality. "There is one God; none exists save God."

The law of impressions challenges our assumptions about individuality. We are constantly being reshaped by our interactions. At the same time, we are reshaping others. Where does one person end and another begin? Fellow _Homo sapiens_ aside, our lives are totally swept up in a whirling welter of beings of all sizes and kinds—visible and invisible, organic and inorganic. We all make each other who we are, and who we are keeps changing. We are all shifting angles of vision by which the One knows Itself.

Think of five people who have influenced you, one by one. Visualize each person in turn. In each case, consider what you have taken from them and what you have refrained from *taking. Observe how each one lives in your spirit in a certain way. Give a nod of acknowledgment to each of them. Now think of five people you have influenced, visualizing them one by one. What did each take from you, and what did each forgo? Give a nod of acknowledgement to these five as well.*

·51·

The soul, so to speak, conceives this impression, an impression that is not only the outline of the personality that has impressed it, but the very essence of that personality that this soul has absorbed. Besides, a soul may not be compared with an object, for the soul is all the life there is. Therefore, it does not only take an impression like a photographic plate, it becomes nurtured with it. The soul is creative, therefore it expresses all that it has absorbed on its way.

Some of the students of Einstein in the world of images are more than students. They are disciples. His spirit has entered them and they are enraptured. They are not merely interested in his theory of special relativity; his entire quest for truth has become their own. They are his spiritual children.

Close your eyes. For a few minutes, give your whole attention to your personality. Inhabit it unreservedly. Be the sum of your influences, experiences, interests, and habits. Now pause and change your orientation. Identify with the soul that preexists this construct and harbors it in its light. See the personality as something acquired, something you can step out of and examine both compassionately and dispassionately.

·52·

The question whether jinns are sent on some mission to human beings on earth may be answered yes. Whether angel or jinn or human, all are intended to play a part in the scheme of the working of the whole universe; and all are used by the wisdom of God for that purpose for which they are created. No doubt the angels are for the angelic plane, jinns for the plane of jinn, yet the inhabitants of the second and third floor also are sometimes sent to the ground floor on an errand whenever it is necessary. The most remarkable thing that one can notice in all these planes of existence is that the beings of all these distinct planes are not imprisoned there by the Creator.

Just as angels sometimes visit the inhabitants of the physical plane, jinns do as well. When they visit, they are called fairies. Little children see fairies easily. An earthly education—at least a modern one—unfortunately means that with each passing year a person becomes less capable of recognizing the fairies in their midst. Nonetheless, the fairies recognize us. Sometimes they play mischief, but mostly they come to lend a hand.

If a jinn doesn't come down to meet you, you may nonetheless go up to meet it. Go out into a garden or park. Every plant has its jinnic and angelic doubles—imaginative and noetic versions of itself. Gaze for a while on a tree, shrub, or herb. Let your breath become slow, deep, and fine. Close your eyes. Now find the plant sightlessly. Let it reveal itself to you in whichever form it chooses. Breathing out, send out a greeting to it. Breathing in, receive its greeting.

·53·

How does a jinn soul communicate with human beings on earth? It focuses itself on the human heart, and experiences all that the human being experiences, and knows all that the human being knows. It is easy for a jinn to do it, because its mind is clear like crystal, and it can accommodate and reflect all that falls within its range of vision.

Jinns are able to look into our hearts. The condition, however, is that they must be in sync with us. A malevolent mind cannot gain that kind of access because its intelligence is not sympathetic or crystalline. Clairvoyance and clairaudience depend on purity of spirit and a motive of goodwill.

Reflect on the intertwined nature of knowledge and love in your experience. Observe how the people for whom you have the most affection are the ones you know the best. Notice how easy it is to summon up the picture of someone you love. In fact, you can do more: you can make yourself present to their soul. In spirit, no one you love will ever be separate from you. There is an inner channel of communication that is always open. It only needs attention.

·54·

One might ask if the souls on their return journey from earth give their experience to the souls coming from above. But what do the souls coming from above give to the souls on their return journey? They can do a great deal, too, for they know the forgotten ways that they have recently traveled through, and the law and custom of the way that the souls on the return journey need learn.

The exchange is mutual. A long and extroverted sojourn in the physical world tends to erase the memory of the inner spheres from the human mind. And so it is that when a recently deceased human regales a curious jinn with tales of the material planet, the jinn is generally more than happy to offer its own local knowledge in return. The jinn welcomingly reintroduces the human to the geography, language, and customs of the world of images.

Imagine meeting a jinn intent on incarnating on earth. What would you tell the jinn about life as it is experienced here? What warning would you give? Which aspects of the embodied life of this planet would you laud? What advice would you offer for navigating the world with grace? Now let the subject turn to the world of images? What questions would you have for the jinn about life there? What are your concerns? What are you especially interested in learning about?

·55·

The question in what manner the jinns can help humans on the earth, may be answered that they are capable of inspiring humans, not with a definite knowledge of things, but with the sense of the knowledge—especially the knowledge of art and beauty, of tone and rhythm, the knowledge of an inventive nature, and sometimes that knowledge that might help in accomplishing great things in life.

The knowledge of the jinns is more theoretical than practical. The jinns aren't so much concerned with nuts and bolts as with noble visions and paradigm shifts. Jinn are consummate system thinkers, designers, and entrepreneurs. But they aren't ones to do heavy lifting.

Reflect on the workings of your mind. Your mind no doubt contains a sizable archive of information. But what is more interesting than the information is how it is organized and the conclusions that stem from it. What is the structure, or cosmology, you have created from all you have seen, heard, read, and discovered? That is to say, what is your worldview? Where are there holes, or blurry patches, in this worldview? Into what regions is it actively expanding and deepening?

·56·

**As the soul passes through the plane of the jinn, it arrives
in the physical spheres. What helps this soul to come to
the physical plane? What opens the way for this new-coming soul to enter physical existence? The souls on earth.**

**What is Cupid? It is the soul that is being born, before it
appears on the physical plane. It is pictured by the wise as
a cupid, an angel. It is an angel, for the soul is the angel.**

Descending jinns are drawn to the human beings who are
to be their parents in the physical world. They are attracted
by the love between the pair, and they augment that love by
means of harmonizing beams they project from above. The
jinn may recognize the shortcoming of one or both of these
prospective parents. In some cases, the jinn foresees that the
couple will not remain together. The jinn may anticipate that
growing up in the care of these parents will not be easy, and
that it will have to burden itself with a complex and fraught
inheritance from them. Nonetheless, the jinn resolves to take
up the challenge. It boldly joins its mind to a human bloodline.

*Think of your mother, if she is known to you. There was a time
when she was not yet your mother. Can you recall your state*

of being prior to being related to her? Can you recollect what drew you to become her child? Consider the same questions with respect to your father, if he is known to you. Why were you attracted to these parents? What legacy have you taken on as a result? What have you chosen to carry forward from them in your life? What have you put aside?

·57·

When the soul is born on earth, its first expression is a cry. Why does it cry? Because it finds itself in a new place that is all strange to it. It finds itself in a captivity that it did not experience before. Every person, every object is something new, something foreign to this soul; but soon this condition passes away.

No sooner do the senses of the infant become acquainted with the outer life, which so continually attracts its attention, than it first becomes interested in breathing the air of the world. Then it becomes interested in hearing the sounds; then it becomes interested in seeing objects before it; then it becomes interested in touching; and then it develops its taste.

An encounter with something new tends to evoke a combination of disquiet and fascination. The strangeness of the world makes a newborn wail with trepidation and chagrin. At the same time, every breath further acclimates it to earth's atmosphere and, one by one, its senses slowly open to what is here.

Imagine this is your first day on the planet. Look out on the world with fresh, innocent, wide-eyed vision. Forget what you know, and meet everything around you anew. Let yourself be perplexed, disconcerted, and wonderstruck by the strangeness and glory of it all.

·58·

The wisdom of nature is perfect, and there is no better vision of divine splendor than an infant in its early infancy. Imagine, if the senses of an infant were as developed as the senses of a grown-up person, it would have lost its mind from the sudden pressure of the physical world falling instantly upon it. Its delicate senses would not be able to withstand the pressure of so many and various and intense activities of this world. How the wisdom behind it, which is the evidence of that divine protector, father and mother: the Creator who is the support and protection of all, works so that gradually the senses of the child develop. The more familiar the infant becomes with life, the more its senses are developed; and the more it knows, the more its mind develops. And it cannot know more than its mind can grasp, so that in every way, the infant is protected, its body and mind both.

Only gradually does the mist of the world resolve itself into clear shapes and forms. Slowly, the vague drone that ruffles the air becomes voices, voices become speech, and speech becomes meaning and connection. Little by little, as if out of an incomprehensible cloud of whirling matter, the here and now comes into focus.

If the totality of what exists were to be suddenly revealed to us, our minds would surely collapse under the endless weight of it all. The veils that obscure our sight are a mercy. As our capacity to assimilate experience grows, more can be shown to us. Looking back over your life, can you see how realizations came to you when you were ready to receive them, and not before? Close your eyes. Acknowledge that there is much more to the universe than is yet apparent. Ask to be shown vaster horizons when you are ready for a further vision of life. At the same time, offer your thankfulness for the protective veils behind which your eyes are slowly building in strength.

·59·

When the soul comes in the physical world, it receives an offering, an offering from the whole universe, an offering from the whole world; and that offering is the body in which to function. It is not offered to the soul by the parents but by the ancestors, by that nation, by that race into which the soul is born, and by the whole human race.

Our physical bodies are not earned, but inherited. Each of us is the heir to an estate more enormous that we can possibly imagine. Our bloodlines carry in their flood triumphs, adversities, elegies, migrations, pleasures, agonies, couplings, recollections, and forgettings beyond count. When the soul enters the body, it is soaked in a river of singing blood.

Stand or sit in front of a mirror. Gaze at your face for a little while. Then defocus your eyes, so that you are looking through the image of your face. Think of your grandparents and other ancestors of whom you have a memory, have seen a photograph, or otherwise have a concept. One by one, let their faces appear from within the lineaments of your face, and let them, as it were, look at themselves in you and through your eyes.

·60·

This body is not only an offering of the human race but it is an outcome of something that the world has produced for ages: a clay that has been kneaded a thousand times over; a clay that was prepared so that in its every development it has become more intelligent, more radiant, and more living; a clay that appeared first in the mineral kingdom, that developed then in the vegetable kingdom, that then appeared in the animal kingdom, and that was finished in the making of that body that is offered to the new-coming soul.

More than a merely human legacy, the body is a planetary and cosmic artifact. Humanity itself is inexplicable except as a product of the workings of the entirety of the earth. Our form is a microcosm of the universe in its totality.

Hold one hand in the other. Consider the mystery of your flesh. The matter you wear has been worn by innumerable powers of earth before you. It has lumbered along on bovine hooves and cropped up in sleek stalks of corn. It has napped in fertile soil and dreamt in limpid streams. When it has departed from your crumbling form it will again tunnel underground, soar in the sky, and do every other imaginable thing under the sun.

·61·

One may ask whether it is not true then, as some scientists say in their biological study, that humanity has risen from the animal kingdom. Certainly it is true, but true in the sense as explained above. In order to come to the world of human beings, a soul need not be an animal and then develop itself in humanity. We need not understand by this that every rock turned into a plant, and every plant became an animal, and every animal turned into a human being. The soul is direct from heaven; it itself functions in a body, and it is this body through which it experiences life on the earth more fully. Rocks and trees and animals, therefore, may not be considered as the ancestors of the soul. It is the body which is the outcome of the working of all these different kingdoms, which are the development of one another.

The body embeds deep time. It is a fragment of the Great Body, and therefore exists in continuous communion with all of the stars, planets, minerals, plants, and animals that make up the universe. The Great Body, in turn, spins in congruence with the Great Mind and the Great Soul. These three together embody the cosmic person called the Spirit of Guidance.

To overcome the estrangement that has set in between ourselves and the living, breathing, pulsing earth, go for a walk. Along the way, every time you encounter a tree, an outcrop of stone, a butterfly, a stream, or anything else you might otherwise tend to see as a mere thing, or object, greet it as a fellow being, or subject. Hail it, silently or out loud, as "sister," "brother," "cousin," "neighbor," or any similar name signaling related-ness and common interests.

·62·

A question arises why must a soul function in a human body—why not in an animal, in a bird, in an insect? The answer is that it does. Souls have functioned in all forms which seem living, however insignificant and small.

What about rocks and mountains, and what about the sea and the river? Where have they come from? And the answer is that nature in general, in its different aspects, is the materialization of that light that is called spirit, the Divine Spirit.

But has it a soul, has everything in nature a soul? There are two things: there are rays and there is light. If the rays are the souls of beings, then the light of the same divine sun is the spirit of the whole of nature. It is the same light; it is the same spirit, only not divided and not distinct as the rays that we call *souls*.

It isn't always easy to see where one being ends and another begins. Does a lone bee have a soul, or does the hive share one in common? If a boulder is hewn in two, are two souls born of what had been one rock-soul?

Spirit pervades and lights up everything. When individuality is observed, we speak of a soul. But no soul is ultimately separable from other souls with which it is related. There are bodies within bodies, minds within minds, and souls within souls—like Russian dolls.

Visit a wild place that holds special meaning for you. It might be a grove in the forest or a tide pool beside the sea. Spend some time in silence, watching and listening. Let the spirit of the place unfurl its presence. See how everything that resides in the place is soaked in a shared atmosphere. Everything that lives there imbibes the distinct elixir of that patch of earth, at the same time infusing its own essence into the mélange. Sense the influence of the place on you, and how that influence deepens the longer you stay there.

·63·

The soul who has already brought with it from the angelic plane a luminous body, and from the plane of jinns a body full of impressions, functions in the end in the human body that the physical plane offers it, and settles for some time in this abode. The human beings, therefore, have all three beings in them: the angel, the jinn, and the human.

When an angel becomes a jinn, in the noetic realm it remains an angel. When a jinn becomes a human, in the imaginative realm it's still a jinn. You might say the jinn is the avatar of the angel, and the human is the avatar of the jinn. Angels may have one, two, or three bodies; jinns may have two or three; but incarnate humans always have three bodies. No human being lacks a jinnic and angelic counterpart.

Go for a walk in the park or on a trail in the countryside. As you walk, shift your perspective. See everything you see from the perspective of the jinn within you. Let the landscape around you become the substance of a reverie. Witness the dynamic geometry and implicit music of the world around you. Then shift your perspective again. See everything now from the vantage point of the angel within you. Enter a world of light in which pure intelligence radiates from all sides, so that every encounter is a confluence of mutually illuminating lights. After some time return to the jinnic perspective, and finally the human perspective, but rather than abandoning the scenes of the angelic and jinnic worlds, keep them in the background.

·64·

What humans acquire on the earth is the experience that they make by the means of their senses, an experience that they themselves make. And it is this experience that humans collect in that accommodation within themselves, which they call the *heart*. And after this is collected, that surface of the heart, which is the collection of their knowledge, they call the *mind*.

The heart is the fruit of the soul's experience of incarnation. Angels have souls and jinns have minds, but only those who have undergone earthly birth develop a heart. The heart is what an angel-jinn who has come to the physical plane makes of its terrestrial discoveries in the light of its celestial intuitions. By means of the heart's knowing, the imaginative realm is endowed with a harvest reaped from the soil of the earth.

Undertake a work of art. It might be, for instance, a painting, a sculpture, or a poem. Before you begin, place your materials in front of you, close your eyes, and envision what you wish to produce. See it, in advance, as clearly as possible. Then set to work. As you work, notice how the object you are creating tends to depart in some degree from what you had foreseen, or how you are elaborating the plan in unexpected ways. Perhaps you are not able to realize the design as exactly as you had hoped. But more interestingly, you might find that in the process of creating what you had envisioned, your imagination progresses and new possibilities are revealed. Your vision is evolving in the course of realizing your aim.

·65·

The question is how far does a person recollect the memory of the angelic world and of the jinn world? One shows the memory of the angelic world and of the jinn world by one's tendencies: the tendency for light, for the truth, for love, for righteousness. One's love of God, the seeking for the truth of life, this all shows the angel in a person. In appreciating beauty, in drawing toward art, in love for music, appreciation for poetry, the tendency to produce, to create, to express—all this shows in a person the sign of the jinn world.

Visions of the imaginative and noetic spheres are inwardly evoked by closing one's eyes and meditatively investigating the unseen. The external witnessing of these spheres, by contrast, happens through a kind of resonance where images and events on earth show an affinity with figures and happenings in the inner planes. A blazing dawn calls up the memory of the landscapes of light that are the home of the soul. An ingenious portrait conveys the lineaments of a jinnic countenance.

In the morning, choose a primordial idea, such as justice, love, majesty, or subtlety. Spend a few minutes with your eyes closed repeating the name of the idea and sensing its meaning. Then open your eyes and resolve, through the course of the day, to recognize the signs and manifestations of the idea wherever they appear. At the end of the day, again close your eyes, repeat the name of the idea, and surround it with all that you have seen and heard that agrees with it.

·66·

The impressions that constitute a person's being, that one has brought as a heritage from the jinn world and that have been imparted from the souls on their way back toward the goal, show also as something different and peculiar to what one's people possess. No doubt it often happens that a child possesses qualities of its ancestors that were perhaps missing in its parents or even two, three generations back. However, this is another heritage, a heritage that is known to us as such.

Our individuality does not consist solely of a legacy from our ancestors and the formative influence of the earthly surroundings we occupy. There is a backstory that is less apparent, but equally important. We do not arrive in the physical world as a blank slate. We come instead as a Rosetta Stone inscribed with angelic and jinnic runes. The hidden prologue prefigures the entire narrative of our life, at once setting fateful limits and opening destined possibilities.

Reflect on your individuality. Notice what you owe to your mother and what you owe to your father. Identify all that you contain that is attributable to ancestors, teachers, friends, and others. See, too, how much of who you are is traceable to the events of your life. But then look further. Are there aspects of your personhood that can be explained in none of these ways? Recognize the traits that you have brought into the world with you. Reflect on these features of yourself. Can you recall, if only vaguely, a set of intuited conditions related to these aspects of yourself–a kind of dimly recalled proto-life now available to you, perhaps, only as a misty auto-mythology?

·67·

I might just as well say that the soul borrows a property: a property from the jinn world and a more concrete property from the physical world. And as it borrows this property, together with this transaction, it takes upon itself the taxation and the obligations besides the responsibility that is attached to this property. Very often the property is not in proper repair and damage has been done to it, and it falls to the soul's lot to repair it. And if there be a mortgage on that property, that becomes the soul's lot. Together with the property, it becomes the owner of the records and the contracts and the papers of that property that it owns.

Home ownership is a considerable responsibility. Maintenance, repairs, taxes, and mortgage payments can sometimes feel overwhelming. You might well ask, do I own my house or does it own me? And yet, we all need a place to live. The questions become, what can I afford and for what purpose am I here?

Before taking on a plethora of worldly obligations it's prudent to identify one's preexisting duties, namely the rights and responsibilities one has already taken on in the inner spheres. A clear accounting becomes essential.

Kneel on the ground with your left knee down and your right knee up. Place your right hand on your right knee, palm up. Recall the highest ideals that motivate you, the substance of your life's mission. In the depths of your mind, trace that mission to a time before time. Resolve to fulfill it. Then place your forehead on the ground and rise up again.

·68·

What makes the soul know of its own existence? Something with which it adorns itself, something that it adopts, possesses, owns, and uses. For instance, what makes the king know that he is a king? His palace, his kingly environment, people standing before him in attendance. If that were all absent, the soul would be no king. Therefore, the king is a palace. It is the consciousness of the environment that makes the soul feel, "I am so-and-so"; what it adorns itself with, that makes it say, "I am this or that." If not, by origin it is something nameless, formless.

Our identity is composed of all that we identify with, consciously or unconsciously. Peel back the layers and, like an onion, at the center of it all we are empty of substance of any kind.

From the smallest subcellular animalcule to the vastest cosmic colossus, we all wear masks on the stage of life. The show must go on!

Close your eyes. Relax, observe your breath flowing in and out, and become still in your body and mind. Now form an image of yourself. See how, in its form, posture, expression, and apparel, that image stands for the various trappings that your soul wears. Gaze on this self with the eyes of your soul. The soul is independent of the conditioned self, but nonetheless has a special rapport with it as the vehicle it has accepted or chosen. As you look at your mortal self with immortal eyes, notice the balance between independence and consideration that marks your soul's attitude toward its avatar. Finally, recombine soul and image and open your eyes.

·69·

On the earth plane, the personality develops out of individuality. The soul is an individual from the moment it has been born on the earth, in the worldly sense of the word. But it becomes a person as it grows, for personality is the development of individuality. And in personality, which is built by building character, is born that spirit that is the rebirth of the soul. The first birth is the birth of human beings, the next birth is the birth of God.

First there is simply the soul. Then comes a cascade of impressions crystalizing in an increasingly fixed concept of selfhood. But the soul shines through the bricolage, and the more it does, the more malleable the construct becomes. Materiality yields fresh sunbursts. Heaven and Earth intertwine and a New Earth comes to light, together with a New Heaven. Creation is renewed and the Creator reappears from the whirling dust.

Reflect on your personal imagination of God—or the Infinite, or the Absolute—however you choose to name the great mystery at the core of being. Observe how concepts seem sadly inadequate to the task of representing the ultimately real. Nonetheless, you may sense behind the concept you tentatively entertain a presence that filters through, reaching toward you as you reach toward it. Throughout the day, keep coming back to the awareness of that presence. How does it strike you when you think of it as He, She, or It? In what relation does it stand toward you when you conceive it as You? What is its dawning place when you perceive it as the eternal subject: I?

·70·

In the angelic world there are no distinct impressions but there is a tuning. The soul is tuned to a certain pitch by the law of vibrations, high or low, according to the impressions it receives from the souls coming back home. In this tuning it gets, so to speak, a tone and a rhythm that directs its path toward the world of the jinn.

Before there was speech there was song, and it's through song that angels communicate. Only, the angels are themselves the songs they sing; they become what they intone. In a duet each singer responds to the melody of their partner, even while making their own mark. In a similar fashion, descending angels resonate with the rhythms and tones of the ascending souls they meet. And so it is that, echoing the songs that ring in their ears, angels are set on a fateful course.

After spending an hour or so with someone, take a moment to reflect on the impact of the contact. Notice how, subtly or not so subtly, you have been swayed by the other's way of being–something hard to put one's finger on, and yet undeniable. If the effect is a welcome one–for instance, one feels calmer, lighter, or more energetic–consciously accept the beneficial influence.

If on the other hand the residue is disagreeable, intentionally shake it off and recenter yourself. Consider at the same time the influence you have communicated to the other.

·71·

Souls in themselves are not different in the angelic world, as it is immediately next to the Divine Being. If there is a difference in the souls there in the angelic world, it is the difference of more or less radiance and a longer or a shorter scope of their run. The law that attracts the souls from the jinn world to the human world is all that they receive from the souls who are bound homeward. In accordance with this, they take their direction toward the physical world.

As the old adage goes, "the color of water is the color of the cup." Once we were all the same color: colorless. Somewhere, we still are. But as the soul has been poured from container to container, we've taken on hues that connect us with some and distinguish us from others. Hence the many tribes, literal and metaphorical, that make up our world.

Think of a color that attracts you. Close your eyes and visualize it. As you inhale, let the color gradually fade away so that at the end of your inhalation only a transparent light remains. As you exhale, let the color you've chosen gradually reappear so that by the end of your exhalation it's again an intensely vivid sight. Continue for a few breaths.

·72·

A person who has studied music and practices through life, will certainly seek the association of musical friends, the artists, the singers, the composers, the lovers of music. Among them one will find one's friends, one's comrades. So a soul from the jinn world is directed according to its love for certain things in the physical world. This shows that God does not thrust certain conditions upon souls going toward manifestation, but in this manner they choose them.

In its descent into individuality, the soul follows a path prepared for it by other souls. But there are always forks in the trail. Why does the soul choose one way rather than another? Free will is a mystery. God doesn't force our hand, but somehow whatever we choose is exactly what was meant to be.

We are guided by our loves. Ask yourself, "What do I love?" Observe how an unaccountable attraction for certain values and preoccupations has shaped your choices throughout life. Witness your deepest affections as an innate configuration within your being, and as the mold of your destiny.

·73·

If one raised one's head from this world of illusion and looked up and asked, "Tell me the secret and the mystery of your creation," one will hear in answer that every thing and being is placed in its place, and each is busy carrying out that work that is to be done in the whole scheme of nature. Life is a symphony, and the action of every person in this symphony is the playing of their part, their particular part in this music.

If there is anything that will give peace, it is the understanding of this.

It can be frustrating dealing with someone whose ideas are diametrically opposed to your own. But do you wish that everyone would think exactly as you do? A world in which everyone thought the same, acted the same, and looked the same would be a terrible bore. All kinds of people, all kinds of species, and all kinds of terrain make for an interesting planet. We each have a part to play in the symphony, and no one can play another's part.

Look closely at something in your house, a gadget for instance, or a piece of furniture. Think of all the people involved in creating it and making it yours: those who chopped the wood or mined the metal, those who crafted the item piece by piece, those who tended the store in which you bought it, and many others. Then think of all the nonhuman agents that had a hand in it, from sunbeams to earthworms. Spare a thought of thankfulness for each who has faithfully done its part.

·74·

The soul comes on earth rich or poor, ripened or unripened, through three phases where either it is enriched or it has lost its opportunity. It takes light from the angelic world, knowledge from the jinn world, and inherits qualities from parents and ancestors.

Of these things that it has collected on its way to its manifestation on the earth, is made that accommodation that is called the *mind*.

The soul is a triple heir. It's the rightful beneficiary of shimmering lucidity from the heavens, penetrating genius from the sphere of ideas, and bittersweet tears from the churning ocean of human striving. But to enjoy its inheritance, the soul must claim it—otherwise the opportunity is lost.

Close your eyes and let your breath become gentle and fine. When you've reached a state of deep calm, ask to be shown the light that was given to you before you were born. After spending some time observing what appears, ask to be shown the seed-thoughts that were communicated to you as the primal light began solidifying in form. After some of the seed-thoughts are revealed and sensed, request to be given a glimpse of the noblest sentiments of your ancestors, and their hopes and prayers for you. When a glimpse has transpired, open your eyes again.

·75·

The body in which the soul functions in the physical plane also contributes to the soul properties of all the worlds that it has belonged to: the mineral kingdom, the vegetable kingdom, and the animal kingdom. It is therefore that a human being is called a universe itself; for in a human being consists all that is in heaven and all that is on the earth.

The molecules that move in us have swum in the bodies of fish, flown in the bodies of birds, flowered in gaudy tropical petals, and slept in slabs of cold granite. Our bones are stone, our blood is water, our heat is fire, and our breath is air. The body is a little universe, the cosmos in miniature.

Go for a walk. As you saunter, give your whole attention to the mineral life around you. Greet the pavement you walk on, and every stone you pass. Be conscious of your skeleton. Think, "I am like you." Another day, go on another walk. This time, give your attention to the plants around you. Hail every tree and bush as a kindred spirit. We all gratefully vegetate under the same sun. On a third day, look for animals. Wherever there is a dog or cat, meet it as a fellow mammal. Treat insects, reptiles, and birds too as kin. Be a beast among beasts, happy to be so.

·76·

And if one were to say what represents the human in oneself, the answer is all things, all attributes of the earth and heaven: the stillness, hardness, and strength of the stone; the fighting nature and tendency to attachment from the animal; the fruitfulness and usefulness of the vegetable kingdom; the inventive and artistic, poetical and musical genius of the world of jinns; the beauty and illumination, love, calm, and peace of the angelic planes—all these things put together make humans. It is therefore that the human soul consists of all, and thus culminates in that purpose for which the whole creation has taken place.

If we have a special knack as human beings, it's the ability to venture into every walk of life. We are built to soar with the angels, to burrow with the moles, and to go everywhere in between. All too often, though, we are prone to forget and confine ourselves to cramped cubicles.

Go out on a walk. As you stroll along, entertain the thought that everything you see around you exists within you, and everything inside you has a counterpart outside. Gradually, let go of the idea of an inside and an outside that are separate from each other. Experience yourself as the universe witnessing itself.

The soul, manifested on the earth, is not at all disconnected with the higher spheres. It lives in all spheres but knows mostly one sphere, ignorant of the other spheres on which it turns its back. Thus the soul becomes deprived of the heavenly bliss and conscious of the troubles and limitations of life on the earth.

To speak of the soul's "descent" is to speak metaphorically. Even now, the soul remains ensconced in the heavens. Meanwhile, however, it has projected its life onto the planes of mind and matter. In doing so, it has so thoroughly and exclusively identified with the frontier of its surveyings that it has all but forgotten its formless home.

Lie on your back on the ground. As you exhale, let your breath expand out in ever-widening circles. As you inhale, let your breath disappear into the innermost recesses of your body. Relax so profoundly that your body seems to unravel and dissolve. Experience a sense of formlessness and imbibe the light pervading the realms beyond form.

·78·

The souls of the seers, of saints and masters and prophets, are conscious of the different spheres. It is therefore that they are connected with the worlds of angels and jinns, and with the spirit of God.

It's not religiosity that makes a holy person holy. Instead, it's the person's vivid awareness of the invisible. Only someone who is in communion with the depths of life can remind us of our own depths. We experience that reminder as a sacred breeze, a zephyr redolent with the fragrance of a forgotten homeland.

Think of a person you met who exuded an aura of sanctity. Recall not so much the outer appearance of the person as the person's uplifting and ennobling atmosphere. For a moment, enfold yourself in that remembered ambience.

· 79 ·

The condition of the ignorant one becomes like a captive who is imprisoned on the first floor of the house and has no access to the other floors of the building; and of the seer, is that the seer has access to all the different floors of the building, wherever the seer may wish to dwell.

Each of us is the inhabitant of a multistoried mansion. From the penthouse, the view overlooking the surrounding city is superb. Most of us, however, remain confined to a single room on the ground floor. Only at night do we visit the other floors, and then only as sleepwalkers. The seer moves between rooms at will, awake, day and night.

Accustom yourself to the thought that, wherever you go, there is always much more than meets the eye. When you enter a room, remind yourself that what is visible is only a fraction of what is present. On other levels of scale, other scenes are unfolding. Notice how in certain states of mind the world around you feels opaque and congested, but when your psyche is tuned to a higher pitch your surroundings seem to translucently recede on all sides toward the infinite. Practice "looking twice" and discerning larger frames of reference at every opportunity.

·80·

The secret of life is that every soul, by its nature, is an *akasha*, an accommodation, and has in it an appetite. And of all that it partakes, it creates of it a cover that surrounds it as a shell; and the life of that shell becomes dependent upon the same substance of which it is made.

The soul cannot see itself, it sees what is around it. It sees that in which it is functioning, and so it enjoys the comforts of that shell that is around it, and experiences the pains and discomforts that belong to that shell. In this way it becomes an exile from its birthland, which is the being of God, which is the Divine Spirit, and seeks, consciously or unconsciously, once again, the happiness and peace of home. God, therefore, is not the goal but the abode of the soul, its real self, its true being.

A walk on the beach presents the eye with shells of many shapes and colors. Closer examination reveals that most are cracked and all are vacant of occupants. With each crashing wave, the scattered shells are further pulverized. Before long, they will turn to sand. Once, however, each was the happy home of a creature. So it is with our bodies and minds; these valued crusts too will become flotsam. Meanwhile the soul remains, and will remain, at one with the sea.

Gently rub your hands over each other, attentively delineating each knuckle and fingernail. Recognize your body as a part of yourself, but a part that is borrowed from the physical world that enwraps it. Remind yourself that your body's material will return to the churning substance of the planet, and your soul will live on.

·81·

There are five spheres of which the soul is capable of being conscious. What are these spheres? These spheres are the different shells, each shell having its own world.

One, *nasut*, is a sphere that is commonly known as the *physical sphere*. How are the comforts and discomforts of this sphere experienced? By the medium of the physical body.

The physical world is the world we experience by means of our five senses. The same place known by other means is not called the physical world. As long as at least one of the five senses is active, the soul stays connected with the physical world. The five senses tend to prove so riveting that other faculties are drowned out. Eventually, however, our physical senses will go dark and we will be compelled to utilize other modes of perception. The transition will come more easily to those that have already well acquainted themselves with alternate channels of discernment.

Practice activating and deactivating each sense in turn. Spend an hour giving your whole attention to what your eyes see. Then close your eyes and rest in sightlessness for ten minutes or so. Similarly attend to, and then suspend, each of your senses, one by one. By this one develops both an appreciation for what the senses bring and the realization that awareness has a life beyond sensation.

·82·

Malakut is the next sphere, the sphere of thought and imagination, where there is a greater freedom and less limitation than one experiences on the physical sphere. A person with thought and imagination can add to life that comfort and beauty that is lacking; and the more real one's imagination becomes, the more conscious of that sphere of mind one proves to be. This sphere of mind is that person's world, not smaller than this world but much larger, a world that can accommodate all that the universe holds; and yet there would be a place in it to be filled.

The perceptions of all minds, human or otherwise, accumulate in malakut. Memories linger there. But equally, the future is prefigured there. Everything that takes shape in the physical world has its prototype in malakut. Whatever can be imagined exists there. In malakut, thoughts are beings. Proximity is not determined there by geographical distance, but instead by degree of attention: "For where your treasure is, there your heart will be also."

Close your eyes. Envision a landscape. Survey the sky of the place in which you find yourself, and the lay of its land. Are there mountains, trees, bodies of water, buildings? Are there people or other animals? Let the scene reveal itself in increasingly vivid detail. Scan the horizons for intimations of beauty and sublimity. As long as your eyes are closed, forget the physical world around you and give your whole attention to the world disclosed in your mind. At last, when you are ready, open your eyes again as though transporting yourself from one realm to another.

·83·

Then there is a third sphere, *jabarut,* a sphere of the soul in which the soul is at home. This sphere the soul of an average person touches a moment. One does not know where one was at that moment—one calls it abstraction. Do they not say, when a person is not listening, that person is not here? Every soul is lifted up to that sphere, even if it be for a moment; and by the light and life with which the soul is charged in that sphere, the soul is enabled to live on this earth the life full of struggles and difficulties. Nothing in the world could give the strength that is needed to live a life on the earth if there were no blessing from heaven reaching one from time to time, of which one is so little aware.

Jabarut is the soul's native land. Its terrain is devoid of shapes and forms. Nothing in Jabarut has a hard edge. And yet there are presences. Each presence is a light that illuminates itself and the lights it encounters. Everything flows into everything else, like breezes or waves interpenetrating.

Find something in your home that holds special meaning for you. It might be a vase you inherited from a grandparent or a faithful potted plant that has long kept you company. Spend some moments gazing on it, then close your eyes. See it now in your mind's eye. Keep visualizing it, and notice how it seems to be looking back at you. It's not only an object of your attention, it's also a subject in its own right. Now let go of the image but continue to sense the object, which you experience as an invisible, but nonetheless palpable, presence. At the same time, experience yourself as a formless, luminous presence. Finally, visualize the image of the object again and then open your eyes and greet its physical form.

·84·

Now there is a question if a soul, by rising to all these spheres, becomes conscious of the jinn world and of the world of angels, or if it only sees, within itself, its self-made world of mind and the spheres of joy and peace in itself. The answer is yes; first it sees its own world by rising to the sphere called *malakut*. It experiences the joy and peace that belong to its own heart and are of its own being. But that is one part of spiritual attainment.

The perpendicular line shows a progress straight within from nasut to malakut, experiencing one's own world within oneself. But that which the horizontal line denotes, is expansion.

The Sufis try to expand as they go on progressing; for it is the largeness of the soul that will accommodate and, in the end, will become all-embracing. Those who will shut themselves up from all other people, however high spiritually these may be, they will not be free in malakut, in the higher sphere. They will have a wall around them, keeping away jinns and even angels when in the angelic world; and so their journey is exclusive. It is therefore that Sufism not only teaches concentration and meditation, which help to make oneself one-pointed, but also the love of God, which is expansion: the opening of the heart to all.

Meditation illuminates the interior of the mind, but the light that floods the psyche remains a cold, austere light unless love infuses it. Love is warm and expansive; its signs are the smile and the tear. The love that is from and for the One overflows in compassion and fellow feeling toward every imaginable being.

Close your eyes and turn your attention toward the crown of your head. Gently breathe in and out a dozen times. With each inhalation turn deeper within, drawn by the crown's magnetism.

Now, with eyes still closed, turn your attention toward the center of your chest. Again, breathe in and out a dozen times. With each exhalation let your heart's instinctive love and compassion radiate out in widening waves, encompassing all that surrounds you.

Finally, breathe a dozen breaths in which you reach inward toward the crown on the inhalation and outward through the chest on the exhalation.

·85·

As there are five elements and five notes recognized by the ancient musicians, so there are five egos, each showing a certain pitch. *Ammara* is the condition of the ego when it is blinded by passions. This shows the animal in human beings, and it is its fullness which is meant by the word *devil*. A person absorbed in passions and emotions is a kind of drunken person, who cannot always see the right: the right way in thinking, saying, or doing. No doubt there are moments when every drunken person is sober, when one realizes one's folly; but very often the longing for being intoxicated again sounds louder in one's head, above the soft murmuring of one's folly.

The imperious self is only concerned with itself and its wants. No one else matters. In fact, to someone in this state of mind, there *is* no one else—every other entity is essentially a thing to be used rather than a person to be respected. Like a drunkard, the imperious self demands the immediate satisfaction of all of its appetites, heedless of the web of mutuality that makes its own life possible.

In daily life, notice when others are in the grip of the imperious self. Rather than taking offense, recognize their state as a spell that has fallen over their soul. Find ways to protect yourself and others without resorting to hostility. Then look further and observe your own patterns of thought and action. Notice when you are slipping into the mentality of the imperious self. In moments of intoxication, pause and draw a breath. Refrain from speaking or acting when under the influence of the imperious self.

·86·

The second, *lawwama*, is the condition of mind that is full of thoughts, good and bad, over which the ego reigns, self-covering the truth. People have bitterness or spite against another, or they have their ways of getting all they desire cleverly, or they find faults with others. They are worried about themselves, anxious over their affairs, troubled about unimportant things. They struggle along through life, being confused by life itself. It is not that their passions and emotions trouble them. What troubles them are their own thoughts and their feelings.

The critical self is a relentless judge. It tries to make sense of the world by dividing everything it comes across into the categories of good and bad. It causes a person to hesitate before acting, which is often for the best, since circumspection preempts all kinds of selfish recklessness. But not all spontaneity is harmful, and the critical self's censoriousness all too often becomes a dour burden. Overthinking tends to spoil creativity and the simple joy of life itself.

At the end of the day, look back over the day's events. Which remembered moments provide you with an abiding sense of satisfaction? Which incidents rankle by contrast? Are there words or actions you wish you could take back? Is there a lesson to learn? Are amends now due to someone you've wronged? Having formed a lucid and constructive assessment of one's errors and a clear picture of the course correction that will be needed tomorrow, let the matter rest. Spend some moments exhaling all feelings of tension and inhaling several deep, fine breaths kindled by the endless love and compassion of the One.

·87·

Then there is the third, *mutma'inna*, those ones who, after their troubles and struggles through life, have arrived at a certain state of balance, of tranquility; and by having arrived at this stage, are beginning to enjoy, to some degree, the happiness that is within. They then concern themselves little with others for their own happiness. They then trouble little with others for their faults. These people know then how to throw off of themselves the load of anxieties and worries that life in the world puts upon one's shoulders. They are then able to harmonize with others, to agree with others; and thus they bring about harmony in themselves, in their atmosphere, and spread harmony around and about themselves, thus harmonizing the whole atmosphere.

The tranquil self doesn't need to look for happiness outside of itself because it has discovered a boundless reservoir of peace within. Unmoved by praise and blame, the tranquil self breathes easy. Its tranquility is a mantle that it spreads over the world.

Think of a compliment that someone has recently given you. Let it blow away in the wind. Now think of a criticism that has been leveled against you. Let it, too, blow away in the wind. Think of yourself simply as a creature made by the Creator. The Creator's breath is in you. Experience the happiness that belongs to the glowing stream of that holy breath.

The fourth is *salima*, the people who have arrived at a point where, though they be in the midst of the life of the world, yet they can rise above it. So life does not trouble them so much as it can trouble others. To these ones, life is of no importance. Yet they fulfill their obligations, their duties in the world, in the same way as everyone else. They are those of whom it may be said that they are in the world but are not of the world. Their love embraces every soul that seeks refuge under their influence. Their peace stills the minds of all they meet, regulating it to the same rhythm as their own. When the soul has arrived at that point, it becomes a blessing to itself and to others.

The peaceful self is a sun of affection. As much light as the sun pours out, its store is never depleted. So it is with the peaceful self. Its love has no agenda. The peaceful self is a grateful witness to all that the One has brought into existence, and a faithful servant.

Consider the affection you have for someone you know. The outer layer, you may find, consists of appreciation for the benefits the person brings to your life. Recognize this type of esteem for what it is, and then put it in brackets. Now sense a deeper layer of regard, an affection that revolves around the virtues you perceive in the person's personality. Having acknowledged this more fundamental source of endearment, suspend it likewise. Finally, look into your heart's core. Can you find there a sentiment that is essentially a bow toward the divine light shining in the person's soul?

·89·

And there is the fifth condition, *'alima*, or God-conscious. Their language becomes different. You cannot understand what their "no" means, what their "yes" means. You cannot very well comprehend the meaning of their smiles or of their tears. They may be sitting before you but they are not there. They may be speaking with you and yet communicating somewhere else. They may be among all and yet absent. You may think you hold them; they are not there. It is these souls that prove the fulfilling of that purpose for which they came on earth. The purpose of the soul is that for which the whole creation has been busied, and it is the fulfillment of that purpose that is called *God-consciousness*.

Like the glass of a window pane, the knowing self is transparent. It yields itself so fully to the light that you can hardly tell that it's there. And yet it *is* there, and it keeps out the cold in the dark of winter.

Dedicate an hour to the intention of God-consciousness. Whatever you see during that hour, see it within the One and see the One within it. See nothing on its own. Later, repeat the exercise, but give it two hours. Still later, three—and so forth until you find yourself spending a full day witnessing the One in everything and everything in the One.

·90·

The questions, why do souls come on earth? why has this creation taken place? what is the purpose of this manifestation? may be answered in one word: satisfaction—for the satisfaction of God. Why is God not satisfied without it? Because God is the only being, and the nature of being is to become conscious of one's being.

The One Being was a hidden treasure and longed to be known. Witnessing requires a witness, so the One Being created the Great Spirit. From the light of the Great Spirit the myriad beings of the universe were brought to life, each tasked with ascertaining the One along an arc peculiar to itself. Every being is a cosmos in miniature, and the horizon of every cosmos is the dawning revelation of God. The frontier is a place of dazzlement.

Contemplate your life's purpose. See how it stands as a ziggurat. At the base, one's attention revolves around food, shelter, and other quotidian requisites of life. Higher up, one is devoted to creativity and being of service. At the top, the purpose of life reveals itself as the moment-by-moment unveiling of the One, the blossoming of the rose of immortal beauty.

·91·

Plainly speaking, through humanity God experiences life to its highest perfection. If anyone asked, "Then what is a human being's duty, if that be the purpose?" the answer is that one's sacred duty is to attain to that perfect consciousness that is one's dharma, one's true religion. In order to perform this duty, humans will have to struggle with themselves, they will have to go through sufferings and pains, they will have many tests and trials to go through; and by making many sacrifices and practicing renunciation, they will attain that consciousness that is God-consciousness, in which resides all perfection.

If the divine glory were to be revealed all at once to everyone, the universe would be instantly reduced to a pile of ash. "No one may see me and live," warns the Creator. We are given to see as much as we can bear. As the heart is stretched, torn, and reborn, more is shown.

Close your eyes, let your breath become fine, and turn your gaze toward your heart. Through the medium of your physical heart, reach into the spiritual heart in the center of your chest.

Give your whole attention to this central heart until it becomes vividly palpable. Whisper to God a silent prayer that expresses what you wish your heart to become.

·92·

But why must people suffer and sacrifice for God? At the end of their suffering and sacrifice, they will find that, though they began to do so for God, in the end it turned out to be all for themselves. It is the foolishly selfish who are selfish, and the wisely selfish who prove to be selfless.

As experience shows, in the long run selfish choices lead to bad ends. Whatever is done altruistically, by contrast, brings a fortunate outcome. Selflessness—or pan-selfism—is ultimately what is best for the self, since the real self of all selves is the Nothing-and-All residing in everything.

When at a crossroads, ask yourself: "Is the course of action that seems to most advantageously advance my personal interests really what is best for my soul? What will be lost by what is gained?"

·93·

Now the question, how may this consciousness be attained? It is to be attained by self-realization. First one must analyze of what one is composed. Humans are composed of spirit and matter. They constitute in themselves the animal world, the mineral world, the vegetable world, the jinn, and the angel; and it is their work to balance it, knowing that neither have they been created to be as spiritual as an angel nor have they been made to be as material as an animal. And when a person strikes the happy medium, that person will certainly tread the path that is meant for a human being to tread, the path that leads straight to the goal.

Realization is the weaving together of apparent contraries: the visible and the invisible, the ephemeral and the eternal, the mundane and the marvelous. Our task is no more to flee from matter than it is to be exclusively engrossed in it. The fulfillment of creation's promise lies in the marriage of heaven and earth. The destined alliance takes place in the innermost chambers of ourselves. We are led to this consummation by the middle road, the path of union.

Close your eyes and place your dominant hand palm-up on your knee. Sense the bones, sinews, nerves, veins, muscles, and skin that compose the intricate anatomy of your hand. Now become aware of yourself as pure awareness, a subtle, boundless light capable of focusing or diffusing itself as it wishes. As you exhale, your hand seems to dissolve into the disembodied light of your invisible being. As you inhale, your light crystallizes in the flesh and bone of your hand.

·94·

Balance is the keynote of spiritual attainment. In order to attain to God-consciousness, the first condition is to make God a reality, that God no longer is an imagination. No sooner is the God-ideal brought to life, than the worshipper of God turns into truth. There is no greater religion than truth. Then truth no longer is one's seeking; then the truth becomes one's being, and in the light of that absolute truth, one finds all knowledge. No question remains unanswered.

How can one possibly conceive a being of infinite proportions? The believer etches a picture of perfection by envisaging an apotheosis of all that is generous and tremendous, naming it the Absolute. The picture remains merely an image, however, until a sweeping turn of consciousness abolishes the Divine as an object of the believer's imagination and reveals it instead as the true subject. God now radiates through the believer's soul as the witness of all that is seen, heard, smelled, tasted, and touched.

Consider your God-ideal, the epitome of the qualities you ascribe to reality in its ultimate essence. Think of this God-ideal as a telescope through which you look out on a mystery beyond reckoning. Then shift your perspective and experience yourself as an object of the divine gaze, seen through the microscope of the World Soul.

·95·

Has the world of the jinn many worlds, as there are planets in our universe? Yes, many, and as different from one another as the planets in our universe are different; yet not so far apart as in our universe, not so out of communication as in our universe.

Our physical universe is the outer reflection of the universe of images, the world of the jinns. Whatever exists here also exists there. Our sun and its nine planets are there, as are the Milky Way and the billions of other galaxies that whirl around the earth.

There are, in fact, more beings in the world of the jinns than here, because everyone here has an imaginative double there, whereas not everyone there has a physical avatar here. For all their numerousness, however, the beings of the jinn world enjoy a rapport that is considerably more vivid than the generally pale mutual familiarity that prevails in the physical world. The closer beings are to the Source, the nearer they are to each other.

Close your eyes and let the focus of your attention expand from the room in which you are sitting to the earth as a whole, then the solar system, then the Milky Way, and finally the entire universe. Let your contemplative gaze subsume billions of galaxies of billions of stars. Consider how all of these planets and stars lead lives beyond their physical forms. Ponder the souls of the stars and galaxies.

·96·

What is the life there? What is it like? It is difficult to explain and difficult to put in words. But, for an example, one might see the difference in the life of the birds that can fly over seas and forests, and fly about over hills and dales, and feel in tune with nature and express their joy in song. Then there are the deer in the woods, dwelling in the caves of the mountains, drinking water at the natural springs, moving about in the open spaces, looking at the horizon from morning till evening, the sun their timekeeper and the moon serving as their torch. And then imagine our lives, the lives of human beings in crowded cities, days in the factories and nights indoors, away from God, away from nature, even away from self, fully absorbed in the struggle of life, an ever-increasing struggle, and there is no end to it. There is the picture before us to imagine what life the angels live in the highest heavens, what life the jinns have in the middle heaven, and to compare them with our life as human beings in our universe.

One may imagine the jinns as being, in some respects, like fish. While we plod along through literal landscapes in these dense forms of ours, the jinns hover and dive among splashing currents of reverie in suits of iridescent scales.

The angels, in turn, may be compared to birds. They stretch their wings and soar, and nothing can weigh them down. Their home is the air, the earthly analog of the Invisible. They are perpetually buoyed in their long glides through the azure of the sky.

Go to a wild place, a place where the hum of passing cars can't be heard even in the distance. Leave behind your social persona and become a force of nature. Sniff the air, prick up your ears, and rove through the dappled light of the forest, fervently giving yourself over to the loamy redolence of the moment.

·97·

What difference is there between the conception of time that we have and the idea of time that is there? There is an incomparable difference. No words will give the exact idea of the comparison between time, but for the sake of convenience, let us say our year is the jinn's hour and the moment of the angel. Are there angels and jinns of longer and shorter lives just as humans on earth? Certainly there are, but the time of their life is not to be compared with that of human beings.

A mayfly lives for a day, a galapagos turtle for a century, and a glass sponge for thousands of years–and all three enjoy full lives in their way. Similarly, a human being appears as a fleeting flash to a jinn, while a jinn strikes an angel as oddly ephemeral. Experiences that convey a sense of timelessness bespeak an angelic mode of perception, even when they transpire within the frame of bodily existence.

Reflect on your life. When did it begin? At the moment of your earliest memory? Consider instead that you have existed since before you can recall, even since before your body was conceived in your mother's womb. Can you intuit, if only distantly, a life preceding your current existence, and equally, a passage that will succeed the present interlude? Think of your present existence not as a self-contained whole so much as the sequel to a previous way of being and the dusky adumbration of a future yet to be revealed. How does your sense of identity shift when you envisage yourself as immortal?

·98·

Are there differences between the jinns and between the angels, as among people of different sorts? Indeed there are, but among the jinns not so many differences as among people, and still less among the angels.

The universe spreads out like a hoary oak, its trunk becoming wandering branches, the branches splaying into offshoots and sprigs unfurling in all directions. Our terrestrial identities take shape at the periphery, where variety reaches its bewildering crescendo. Closer to the common trunk, prevailing resemblances point to the shared origin of all beings.

Each of us is a self among many selves. How do the various markings of your individuality distinguish you from others? Conversely, what commonalities link you with fellow humans and indeed animals of various species? If you cannot agree with someone at the level of personal opinion, can you discover congruence, and even a sense of oneness, at the level of primal awareness?

·99·

The construction of the body is made to make all that is perceptible clear, for by nature, the body is the vehicle of the intelligence or of the soul, by which it experiences life fully. But as humans have lived, for generations, an increasing life of artificiality, they have moved further and further from nature. Therefore, this vehicle, which was made a perfect instrument to experience life fully, has become more and more incapable of attaining that object. It is this incapability of experiencing life fully and that innate desire for the experience of life that makes the soul strive for spiritual attainment.

The body is not the soul's prison, but its prism. By means of the body the soul enjoys an interactive and panoramic immersion in the world of embodied things. But the subtle capacities of the body are all too often dulled and blunted by the creeping miasmas of collective illusion that infiltrate the nervous system and clog its finer sensibilities.

Close your eyes and become aware of your breath. As you exhale, sweep out the dust that has accumulated within yourself. Let each exhalation empty you more completely. Eliminate the grime from each of your senses in turn: touch, taste, smell, hearing, and sight. Inhaling, draw in fresh air and purifying beams of sunlight. Open your eyes to a renewed world.

·100·

What one does not know, one thinks does not exist. In this is to be found the reason for materialism. But the tendency toward spiritual realization remains there, as an innate desire that is consciously or unconsciously felt by every soul, whether spiritual or material. It is therefore that a material person has a silent craving in the heart to probe the depth of the spiritual ideal that that person disowns.

When an ossified spirit forgets or denies the reality of the numinous, it nonetheless remains a spirit. Sooner or later all beings will discover themselves and the One to whom they belong. Meanwhile, every earthly throat knows a thirst that no luscious morsel, no gilded crown, and no tome of lore can slake, a thirst for the Water of Life that flows in the dark recesses where reason and ego cannot go.

Turning within, plumb the deepest wells of your awareness in search of the Ideal, the impress of divinity that marks the world with holiness. Accept that you will never be able to adequately conceptualize the Ideal in words, or even in images. Intuit the Ideal as something that is more factually real than the furniture in your room, and yet endlessly mysterious in its amorphous splendor.

·101·

It is the same sense that hears, sees, smells, tastes, and feels touch; but because it experiences life through different organs, the one sense is divided into five senses. The depth of that sense, which is the inner sense, is more subtle than a person can imagine. When that sense finds a free expression, it does not only experience life more keenly by the help of the organs of the senses, but it becomes independent of the organs of the senses.

It's not the eye that sees or the ears that hear. Eyes and ears are instruments, like binoculars or a hearing aid. It's the common sense that perceives whatever is perceived, and the five senses are at its dutiful agents. As a matter of habit, the common sense projects itself through the senses with a view to navigating and manipulating the external world. In doing so, it loses touch with its own quiddity. However, if it so chooses, it is capable of doubling back and bubbling up like a fountain.

Imagine a light surrounding and pervading your body. Recognize this light as the seat of your intelligence. One by one, withdraw your senses into the light: touch, taste, smell, hearing, and sight. For a few moments, reside in the light and carefully observe your perceptions, perceptions no longer restricted to the input of the senses. Finally, return to your senses one by one—sight, hearing, smell, taste, and touch—investing each in turn with the light you have uncovered within.

·102·

There is nothing in this world that does not speak. Every thing and every being is continually calling out its nature, its character, and its secret. And the more the inner sense is open, the more it becomes capable of hearing the voice of all things. In every person this sense is, for the greater part, hidden, buried; and its being buried gives it discomfort, for it is something that is living—the only living being there is. When once this inner sense has broken the walls around it that keep it closed, it breathes freedom; and that happiness, which is the soul's own property, the soul attains.

Everything is continuously communicating its secret to all who will listen. But there are few listeners. Those who might have otherwise been listening are usually giving their attention instead to a voice-over buzzing in their brain. Only when the drone of the commentary ends does the music of listening begin.

Turn off your devices and enter a state of silence. Let the silence soak into your mind and heart. Sit in front of a natural thing— a stone or a tree, for instance. Exhale with the thought, "May I hear you." Inhaling, listen. Put aside all preconceptions. What message is communicated to you on the current of your breath?

·103·

Every discomfort, from whatever source it comes, comes from the lack of understanding. The more the inner sense is covered, the more it finds itself in obscurity. It is therefore that the sign of the enlightened soul is that readiness to understand. Therefore, they are easy to reconcile with; when one can understand oneself better, one can make another person understand better also. But when one is perplexed oneself, instead of making another person understand, one confuses that other. In this way differences are produced.

There are people with whom conversation is easy. In fact, words aren't even necessary with them; they understand you implicitly, as though they can see straight into your soul. With people of this kind you can relax your defenses and be completely at ease. Your heart opens in their presence the way a heliotrope opens to the sun.

When you wake up in the morning, set the intention to sincerely attempt to understand everyone you encounter in the course of the day. Throughout the day, whenever you meet someone, make yourself conscious of their soul. Avoid all unnecessary arguments. Look for the best in everyone at every moment.

·104·

As in a mirror one sees oneself reflected, so this body stands as a mirror in which every experience of the outer life is reflected and is made clear. If the mirror is dusty, it does not show the image clearly; so the experience of life is not clear when the body is not looked after according to the spiritual point of view.

The Sufis say that the body is the temple of God, but the right interpretation of this saying is that the body is made to be the temple of God. A temple cannot be called a temple of God if God is not brought and placed there.

This terrene body we wear is a marvel of cosmological artistry. To have it in one's trust is an honor. It follows that the care and cultivation of the body as an instrument of being and knowing is a matter of spiritual conscience. Our bodies exist for the fulness of our soul's realization.

In the morning, look at yourself in the mirror. Say to yourself: In this same way that this mirror reflects my face and form, may my body–with its eyes and ears and all of its senses–clearly reflect the face and form of all those I meet. May it be a well-polished mirror-temple in which the light of the divine presence shines brightly.

·105·

The soul manifests in this world in order that it may experience the different phases of the manifestation, and yet may not lose its way and be lost but may attain its original freedom, in addition to the experience and knowledge it has gained in this world.

A person may be intelligent, clever, learned, good, or pious, and yet one's sense of perception may not be fully awake. It must be remembered, as the first principle of life, that manifestation was destined for a keener observation of life within and without.

The soul's essential task is to witness being. First the soul is a witness to the world of lights, then it's a witness to the world of forms, and finally it becomes a witness to the world of bodies. At each step, the soul has a tendency to forget what it saw before. When it learns to see body, form, and light in unison, it has prepared itself for the unveiling of the divine oneness.

Wisdom is born of the marriage of knowledge and simplicity. When you find yourself excited by a curiosity that stimulates your mind, seek out the stillness of pure awareness and let your fascination float in it. Conversely, when you find your-self serenely reposing in sheer equanimity, reach out from that golden calm and send an antenna into the world around you.

·106·

As there are different organs of the senses, so there are the centers of inner perception. The Sufis have called the five centers of inner perception by the terms *'arsh, kursi, lawh, qalam, 'arsh al-a'zam*. These centers denote seats of intuitive faculties.

Two among these centers are of great importance: the heart and the head. The head without the heart shows dry intellect; the heart without the head represents an unbalanced condition. The balance is the use of both these faculties. The whole Sufi training is based on this principle.

The five primary subtle centers are situated in the crown, the forehead, the middle of the chest, the belly, and the tailbone. Among these, the centers in the head and chest are most consequential. The thinking of the brain is balanced by the feeling of the heart, and vice versa. Too much of one or the other makes a person lopsided.

Close your eyes and let your breath soften and deepen. Imagine a glowing point in the center of your chest. Now imagine another glowing point, this one situated behind your forehead. Inhaling, trace an energetic current up from the first point to the second. Exhaling, trace the link in the opposite direction. Observe the two centers entering into mutual accord. Continue for several breaths, then open your eyes.

·107·

The centers may be likened to the space that one finds in the apple. It is an _akasha_, an accommodation, where not only smell, touch, seeing, and hearing are perceived, but even the thought and feeling of another is perceived, the condition in the atmosphere is perceived, the pleasure and displeasure of one's fellow human is perceived. And if the sense of perception is keener, then even the past, present, and future can be perceived. When a person does not perceive it, by this it does not mean that it is foreign to that person's nature. It only means the soul is not wakened to that perception.

Dense organs sense dense sensations and subtle organs sense subtle sensations. The invisible knows the Invisible. To perceive what is less than obvious one has to become less thickheaded, more supple and spacious.

Close your eyes and turn within. Relax the constriction in your tailbone by imagining yourself untying an invisible knot there. When a sense of spaciousness arises, shift your attention to your belly and again imagine untying a knot. Proceed likewise in your chest, your forehead, and your crown.

·108·

The absence of such fine perception naturally causes depression and confusion, for the soul longs for a keener perception and feels confused, and at times agitated, owing to the lack of a fuller perception. This, generally, is the cause hidden in many souls who feel uncomfortable; and the life we live, a life of artificiality, works against it. We do not need to read the ancient traditions to find out the truth about it. Today the people who live a less artificial life, a more simple life, a life in nature—their intuitive faculties are more keen, and they show a greater happiness.

For better or worse, one's way of life always leaves its mark on one's body and mind. We are affected more than we know by the places we occupy, the tools we use, and the food and drink we consume. Modern life favors efficiency, but what is convenient is not always satisfying or even benign.

After each of the habitual actions that make up your day, pause and ask yourself: "How did the action I've just performed, and the way in which I did it, affect my body, mind, and soul? What part of me readily took part in the activity, and what part stood apart, excluded? What does the alienated element in me need in order to come back into the fold?"

·109·

The physical body is made of matter, its sustenance is matter. But the centers of perception, located in the physical body where no nourishment can reach, can be reached by that which is drawn in through the breath, the fine substance that is not even visible. In the language of the mystics it is called *nur*, which is light.

Breath is a swing. By means of it, as we know, oxygen is carried into the body and carbon dioxide is carried out. But the swing carries more than air molecules. It also carries the luminous pulsations that pour down from the heavens. These vibrations feed the invisible subtle centers that the body encases. Just as physical organs make up the anatomy of the body of flesh and blood, the subtle centers are the constituents of a body of light.

Close your eyes and breathe with gentle awareness. Be conscious of the billions of stars that surround the earth. Visualize the flashing rays of these countless stars streaming down through earth's atmosphere. Let your skin soak up the light that is coming down. Drench yourself in starlight, right down to the marrow of your bones.

·110·

The body not only wants food but also breath, in other words, vibration; and that vibration is given to it by the repetition of sacred words. The sounds and vowels and the composition of the sacred words is chemical; and it is this chemistry that was called by the ancient philosophers, *chemia* or *alchemia*.

A newborn baby is nurtured as much by its mother's whispered endearments and lullabies as by her milk. All words produce an effect, but the most powerful ones are the mantric words passed down the ages from revealed sources. When rhythmically repeated at regular intervals, these words alter the chemical composition of the body and let in brilliant shafts of light.

Divine names or mantric syllables are best received from people of remembrance. When you have the blessing of such a person to recite a word of this kind, resolve to repeat it every day at the same time. Let everything disappear from your mind except the holy word. As it reverberates through your body, feel it penetrating into the deepest recesses of your existence, imparting a peace and joy that can hardly be described.

· 111 ·

These centers are the akashas, or domes, where every sound has its re-echo; and the re-echo, once produced in this akasha, reaches all other akashas that exist within and without. Therefore, the repetition of a sacred word has not only to do with oneself and one's life, but it spreads and rises higher than we can imagine, and wider than humans can perceive. Verily, every movement has its influence upon every atom of the universe; every action sets to movement every atom of the universe.

Agitation has a way of leaping from person to person like a rampant virus. But peace of mind also spreads. You transmit what you attune to. By transmitting peace, you make peace more available to those who come within your ambit. Those you've influenced in turn influence others. By embodying a state, you promote that state within the body of the World Soul.

Immediately after an encounter with someone, notice the residue that remains from the exchange. Are you left standing in a gloomy cloud? If so, shake off the haze before moving on, and when you do, don't look back. Or was the meeting of an elevating kind—is your system now buzzing with new light and life? If so, gratefully digest the welcome influx of magnetism and resolve to pass on the favor wherever you are in the hours ahead.

·112·

Among those who tread the mystical path, one finds many who are sensitive and become more sensitive as they develop spiritually. To the uninitiated, the sensitiveness of a person of mystical temperament might seem peculiar. At the same time, when it is developed by spiritual training, the sensitiveness is under control. This manifests as the first thing in the life of a seer.

The fine and far-reaching perceptive powers of poets and visionaries frequently make them receptive to the point of hypersensitivity. Spiritual training sustains and even doubles this congenital alertness, but at the same time tethers it to a constantly deepening familiarity with the ubiquitous presence of the One. Lacking a coherent center, untutored sensitivity can easily veer into nervousness and depression. The receptivity of an adept, by contrast, has at its core an unshakable confidence in Being.

At the beginning of the day, dedicate your mind and heart to the One. Think, "Whatever I am shown today, You will be the witness. My senses are Your instruments." Throughout the day, feel the gaze of the One threading through your glance. At the end of the day, offer up all of your experiences to the One. Keep nothing to yourself.

·113·

When the centers in the body are awakened and at work, then the soul experiences life more clearly; and naturally, clouds that give depression clear away. The soul begins to look forward to life with hope and trust and with courage, and thus attains that power and understanding that is needed to struggle through life.

The body within the body–the body of light–mediates between the body and the mind. When the light body languishes in neglect, body and mind both suffer. When it flourishes, body and mind are lifted into a mutually enhancing accord.

Close your eyes and turn your attention to the five major subtle centers one by one: the tailbone, the belly, the middle of the chest, the forehead, and the crown. In each center invoke the name of God in any language, and ask for light. With fine awareness, tend to what is dawning in each center in turn.

·114·

There is no doubt that, as the sight becomes keen, first, the finer colors of different elements working in nature manifest to view. Next, the atmosphere that is created around one, which is composed of semi-material atoms, becomes manifest to one's eyes. This is what is called the *aura*. The different colors of the aura denote the meaning of it, for there is nothing in this world that is without meaning. The one who pursues the meaning of life in all its aspects hears again, in the end, the word that was once lost for one.

Different ways of looking disclose different scenes. Tracing edges brings into view an assortment of bounded, self-contained objects. Surveying horizons unveils sweeping panoramas bathed in a common sky. Gazing into the space between things reveals glints of the rarely noticed subtle light that circulates between bodies—but only if one's eyes are kept close to the soul and are therefore hawkishly keen. The scintillating colors seen in the air herald the particular elements of the moment. Yellow announces earth; green, water; red, fire; and blue, air. Within the swirl of elemental colors, primal ideas loom. From the depths of the ideas, the creative speech of the One rings out.

In moments of leisure, withdraw your glance from the contours of the objects around you and gaze into the air. At first it might feel awkward to lack a supporting surface on which to rest your focus. In time, however, you may find that you are able to suspend your focus in the air with ease. When interacting with others, direct your attention less to their features and more to the space between you. Carefully observe the character of the light that reaches you through that space.

·115·

The mind is not necessarily the brain. Mind is a capacity, an akasha, that contains all the experiences we make in life. It has all the impressions we gain through our five senses. It is not in the body, it is around the body. But the centers of perception reflect every thought and feeling, and thus one feels that mind is within oneself. In point of fact, the body is in the mind, within the mind; not the mind within the body. As the eye sees an object before it and reflects it, so the centers of perception reflect every thought and feeling.

Radio waves are all around, but they remain unheard unless a radio converts them into audible sounds. Similarly, bodies are the place-bound instruments of minds that are, in themselves, diffuse. The nervous system tunes into the condition of the mind and communicates its inclinations across the body's breadth. Each plexus is in contact with a certain mental factor.

Throughout the day, instead of thinking of yourself as your body, think of yourself as your mind. Rather than imagining your mind as somehow occupying your brain, conceive of it as the invisible expanse of awareness inside of which your body lives and moves. It pervades not only the entirety of your body, but everything you encounter. Everything you have ever seen or known lives on in it.

·116·

Though the mind experiences life even through the material organs of the senses, still the mind is more perceptive and can experience life and its different aspects standing aside from the body. In other words, the mind can see for itself, it can hear, even without the eyes and the ears; for the mind has its own eyes and ears. Though the mind needs the physical eyes and ears to see and hear, still there are things that the physical eyes cannot see and the physical ears cannot hear—the mind sees and hears them. The more independent the mind is made of the outer senses, the more freely the mind perceives life and becomes capable of using the outer senses, the organs of the senses, to their best advantage.

In the daytime the mind looks out through the outer senses, but at night it makes use of different senses. In dreams all kinds of sights appear, some ordinary and others phantasmagoric. Sometimes a dream gives an indication of something happening elsewhere in the world, something one's waking senses were not privy to. Seeing and hearing do not end when the eyes and ears close. Even in daylight, imagination is constant. Nothing can be done without first envisioning it.

Close your eyes, relax, and turn within. Think of someone you know and dearly love. Picture their face and form, letting the portrait etch itself sharply in your mind. Whether this person is currently in the room next door, on the other side of the world, or in the world beyond, it makes no difference—this is someone who, in all circumstances, has a permanent place within your mind and heart. If you attend closely enough to the inner image, it comes to life. The one toward whom you are turning turns toward you.

·117·

The question, has the mind a form? may be answered, yes, the mind has the same form with which the soul is most impressed. The question, what form is there with which the soul is most impressed? may be answered, one's own form. That is why, when one says "I," one identifies with the form that is most impressed upon the mind, and that is one's own.

But the mind is a world in itself, a magic world, a world which can be more easily changed, more quickly altered compared with the physical form. The phenomenon of the mind is so great, and such wonders can be performed if one had the key of the mind in one's hand.

The body and mind each impress themselves on the other. If the mind is anxious, it knits the brow and engraves worry lines on it. The mind might bend the back or it might straighten it. It might darken the eyes or illuminate them.

The body impresses the mind by suggesting an identity. When we dream, we see ourselves more or less as we are when our eyes are open. This is only because the mind has come under the body's spell. The more the mind realizes its own life, the more freedom it has in determining the lineaments of its dream body.

Look into a mirror, gaze at your reflection, and then close your eyes. With eyes closed, continue to see your face before you. Now spend a few moments silently contemplating your highest and most sacred ideal. Again inspect your face with your mind's eye. How has the glow of your contemplation modified its contours?

·118·

The real place where the heavens are made is within the human being. The mind is made of all one learns, one experiences, one loves, and one remembers. It is therefore that one is that which the mind contains. If the mind contains a sorrow, one is sorrowful; if the mind contains joy, one is joyous; if it contains success, one is successful. If it contains failure, failure awaits one; everywhere a person may move, that person will find failure. The mind is an accommodation in which one collects all that one learns and experiences in life.

To dig in the earth is to travel back in time. Near the surface of the winter ground, the roots of last year's herbage sprawl in a tangle. Deeper down there may be an old arrowhead, and deeper still, a brontosaurus bone. The mind is similarly built up layer by layer. Every phase of life bequeaths its soil and timeworn heirlooms. The past mounts up as the foundation on which the present finds its feet.

Look back on the story of your life. The past persists as the substance of your mind. Linger over an event that has shaped not only the course of your life, but also your way of being. Discern how narrative becomes self: you are the unfolding adventure of your soul's journey—and at the same time, you are simply the soul itself.

·119·

The mind is not only the treasure house of all one learns, but creative by nature. The mind improvises upon what it learns and creates, not only in imagination, but it finishes its task when the imagination becomes materialized. The heavens or the infernal regions—all are the creations of the mind, and all are experienced in the mind.

We have choices. Not only is the mind the sum of its experiences, it is also the pattern that arranges the experiences, foregrounding some and downplaying others. In fact, it does more than this. It molds the forms it's given to make new forms. A mind whose heart is set on heaven can turn devils into angels with a look.

Reflect on the way in which your mind and heart have been digesting the circumstances of the last year. There is likely new information to reckon with—is your perspective correspondingly evolving? Observe how your psyche is, or isn't, adjusting its structure to accommodate previously unconsidered realities and possibilities. Experiment with shifts in perspective. For instance, summon up the most illuminating insight discernible on your mind's horizon together with the thorniest problem in your life, and consider how the two mental images might meaningfully interface.

·120·

But there is the question, is the body not born with a mind? Did the mind not exist before the body? Yes, it did exist as an akasha, an accommodation. The first design of that akasha is molded upon the impression that falls deeply upon the soul, the soul coming toward manifestation from the infinite spirit. It is this impression that has helped this first mold of the mind to be formed, to manifest its original nature and character through the body with which it is connected and identified.

Between the gates of spirit and matter, the soul passes through the realm of imagination and acquires the foundations of a mind yet to be built. These foundations consist of impressions collected from the disembodied landscapes and preincarnate encounters through which it moves. Here lies the original ground of the human personality.

Consider your personal character and inclinations. Much can be explained by tallying the various influences that have shaped your life. Looking back, however, you may notice that from the very beginning not all external factors have equally compelled you. You have readily heeded some calls and consistently ignored others. Within you are predilections that precede and inform the events of your life, rather than arising as products thereof. What do these predilections imply about your soul's passage through the realm of imagination in its journey to the shore of matter?

·121·

If it happens to be the impression of one personality falling upon the mind going toward manifestation, in the life of that person, the distinct character of a certain personality who lived in the past will show clearly. It is in this that the secret of the doctrine of reincarnation, which the Hindus have held, can be recognized.

As certain souls make their way toward the frontier of manifestation and others wend their course back to the Source, it's to be expected that there will be chance meetings at various crossroads and way stations along the way. In these encounters, each soul naturally speaks of what it knows: the descending soul conveys something of the innocence of the spheres from which it has recently come, and the ascending soul communicates a portion of its terrestrial knowledge. Afterward, the earthbound soul goes its way bearing in its chest a growing fascination with all things incarnate and experiential, while the rising soul departs lighter of spirit and eager to be once more among the angels of the upper reaches.

Close your eyes, refine your breath, and turn within. Imagine coming face-to-face with an angel approaching the physical

world and preparing to undergo birth. How does the angel ap-
pear to you, and how do you imagine you appear to its eyes?
What is worth relating to a newly arriving soul about this world
and life as you know it?

·122·

All we see before our eyes, all the objects made by human skill, conditions brought about in life, favorable or unfavorable, they are all the creation of the human mind—of one mind or of many minds. One's failures in life, together with the impression of limitation that humans have, keep one ignorant of that great power that is hidden in the mind.

Everything visible in the physical world is the effect of a cause in the world of images. Shapes molded in material clay have first been sculpted in the clay of vision. Earth's matter is susceptible to every conceivable form. Hence, within the broad bounds of Nature's law—or shall we say her habits—everything is possible. Imagination is the key.

As a contemplation, reflect on the good fortune of being alive on earth and having in your soul's keeping a mind and a body. Recognize the discouragement that sometimes haunts you as nothing but a shadow, and align yourself with the luminous thought of all-possibility. Consider how, by means of mental and physical action, you are constantly creating your life, a life that will always manifest your imagination and intention. Who do you wish to be? What do you wish to bring into being?

·123·

A person sees the folly of another and wishes to judge another when the sense of justice is not wide awake. Those whose personalities have brought comfort and healing to their fellows were the ones who only used the faculty of justice to judge themselves, who tried to correct themselves of their own follies and, being engaged in correcting themselves, had hardly time in their life to judge another.

One's mind is one's personal work of art. To spend time sizing up others' failings is to miss the chance to enlarge one's own successes. Time is of the essence, and success is only in God.

Whenever you are inclined to criticize someone, reflect on how the flaw that you condemn exists to some extent within yourself also. Resolve to prune that tendency in your mind. Conversely, whenever you see someone act admirably, recognize that you are fully capable of the same behavior and resolve to put it into practice.

·124·

The question, then why does not all we think come true; why is all we wish not always realized? may be answered that by our limitedness, we, so to speak, bury the divine creative power in our mind. Life confuses us so much that there is hardly, among a thousand, one who really knows what one wants.

Why don't our wishes come true? Because we don't know what we wish for. We try to go north and south at the same time, and end up going nowhere. Focus brings fulfillment.

Identify your greatest desire. Observe how other desires undermine it. Sooner or later, a choice will be necessary. Subsume all lesser desires within your great desire. Let go of any wants that can't be reconciled with your master passion. Reiterate your true wish to yourself every morning and evening, and align your whole life to its attainment. Along the way, have respect for the heart's wishes of everyone with whom you share your life.

·125·

With all the power of the mind, one thing must be remembered: "Man proposes, God disposes" will always prove true when human desire stands against the will of God Almighty. Therefore, the path of the saints in life has been to seek, with resignation, the will of God, and in this way swim with the tide, so that with the accomplishment of their wish, the purpose of God may be fulfilled.

The divine will is a fast-flowing river, and the human will is a slender but useful paddle. Rowing upstream is hopeless. The trick is not to oppose the current but to navigate it with deftness so that the journey is smooth and free of avoidable collisions.

Think of the circumstances of your life. There are certain facts that cannot be altered. Consider an especially challenging example. Since one's kismet is a given, what lies in your power is to choose the attitude you wish to adopt in relation to it, and the course of action that now seems best. Many options remain on the table, and a phoenix may be waiting in the ashes.

·126·

The mind has five different aspects. These are distinguished as the different departments of the mind, which have their own work to do. First, the heart, which feels and which contains the four other aspects of mind in itself. Second, the mind, which creates thought and imagination. Third, memory. Fourth, the will that holds the thought. And fifth is the ego, that conception of mind that claims, "I."

The mind is a hand: sensation is the little finger, imagination the ring finger, memory the middle finger, will the index finger, and the self the thumb. A perception suggests a conception, which in turn stimulates a recollection. The will now determines a response, acting, as always, on behalf of the self. And who is the self? Finding the answer to that question is the great task of our lives. An emptiness exists there, but one in which there is always more to discover.

Close your eyes and refine your breath. Observe the findings of your five senses. For a few moments, give your whole attention to what your body feels. Then drop sensation altogether– or rather, suspend it for a little while. Turn to your thoughts.

Witness their shapes, their flow. Spend some time surveying the constantly shifting scene unfolding in your mind. Then call a halt to image-making. Travel back to a time and place that beckons to you. Relive the moment in vivid colors. Enjoy the presence of the past; then let it go. See how it is your volition that shifts your focus here or there. For a few moments, turn your will in on itself. Inhabit the power of your resolve. At last, suspend that too. Enter into your selfhood. The social persona is its façade; its interior is a pure expanse of I-ness. It's a self-luminous light that knows itself by itself. After a little while, resume willpower, then memory, then imagination, and finally sensation.

·127·

The body is a vehicle of the mind and is also made by the mind—not the same mind, but by other minds. The child does not only inherit the form and features of its parents and ancestors, but their nature and character, in other words, their mind, which molds its mind and body.

What a remarkable relic the body is. This marvel we inhabit is nothing less than a living, breathing record of the lives of its innumerable precursors, not to mention the countless animals, plants, minerals, and stars folded into the forms of those forebears. To inherit such a thing is an acute trust.

The body presents the soul with a set of possibilities, all of them rooted in deep history. Each possibility exerts a compelling persuasive power, though none is so absolute as to lock the soul into a fixed predestination. Even in the body, the soul remains free.

Think of an ancestor with whom you have some familiarity. Sense this forerunner with you, within you, inside your skin. For a moment, enter into the ancestor's character and field of vision. Let your respective hearts beat in tandem across the gulf of elapsed time. At last, return to your private self, but doing so, acknowledge that the other will always be with you.

·128·

The awakened mind makes the body sensitive to all different feelings. The sleeping mind makes the body drowsy. At the same time, the fineness of the body has its influence in making the mind finer; and the denseness of the body makes the mind dense.

When there is harmony between the mind and the body, health is secure and affairs will come right. The secret of mysticism, therefore, is to feel, think, speak, and act at the same time; for then, all that is said or felt or done becomes perfect.

If the mind is a hand, the body is its glove. The glove fits the hand more or less snugly and serves it well for the most part, particularly when rough surfaces need handling. Of course, the glove only moves when the hand moves. It's warm when the hand is warm, and cold when the hand is cold. The glove also transmits its condition to the hand. If it gets wet or catches fire, the hand is liable to get damp or suffer a burn.

Close your eyes and breathe with awareness. Think of your breath as a pulsing link between your visible body and your invisible mind. As you inhale, survey your physical sensations and draw them in. Gather into the net of your mind every passing flicker that registers in your nervous system. Now, at the culmination of your inhalation, briefly pause. The mind is not only a repository for internalized sensations; it has its own color and cohesion. As you exhale, watch the tenor of your mind infuse itself into your body. Not a single cell remains untouched.

·129·

The different minds in the world may be likened to various mirrors, capable of projecting reflections and subject to reflect all that falls upon them. No one, however great in wisdom and power, can claim being free from influences. The only difference between the wise and foolish is that the wise one turns the back to what one must not reflect; the foolish one does not only reflect the undesirable thought but, most proudly, owns it.

To shift metaphors: not everything edible is nutritious. Those who choose their food carefully enjoy better health. In the same way, not all impressions equally nourish the mind. A bad diet of thought dims the psyche's brilliance. No one can entirely evade unsavory influences, but the wise know what to consume and what to toss in the scrap bin for composting.

Before going to sleep, look back on the impressions that have touched your mind in the course of the day. Carry into the night only those that you find yourself moved to preserve. Let the others go.

Gradually develop the habit of selecting between impressions as they happen. Instead of taking it to heart when someone acts provocatively, consider it a quirk on their part, shake it off, and keep going.

·130·

No thought ever born of the mind, be it even for a second, is lost. Thought has its birth and death as a living being, and the life of the thought is incomparably longer than that of the living beings in the physical body. The relation of the thought that is created by a certain mind, to that mind, is that of the child to its parents. It is therefore that humans are responsible not only for their actions, but even for their thoughts.

Our thoughts are our children. They gain lives of their own and pursue destinies in tune with the impulses we have planted in them. There is a place where physical objects are pale and blurry things, but ideas, the offspring of glowing minds, are bright and swift-footed creatures. That place is here—it takes only a second look to see it.

Consider an image or idea that has been living and growing in your mind in recent weeks. If it's a thought you genuinely wish to empower, close your eyes and give your full attention to it for a few minutes. Take care not to restrict yourself to the idea as you already conceive it. Let it reveal itself with increasing fullness, so that it more and more takes on the character of a living being of a sort. Continue in this way for some time. When the idea has a strong, clear, and abiding presence, turn to another idea and nurture it too, and then another, so that a constellation of living ideas crystallizes in the center of your mind. Whenever you wish, you can call to mind the constellation and rotate it, witnessing each idea in turn and the pattern that unites them all.

·131·

It would not be an exaggeration if one called the mind a world. It is the world that one makes in which one will make one's life in the hereafter, as a spider weaves its web to live in.

The place where material objects are distant but thought forms are near is the region in which our minds will live and move when the body and mind part ways. How advantageous, therefore, to get to know the lay of its land now. To do so is to preempt death and remove its sting. We will live longer in the home we have constructed out of thought and feeling than in any house built of bricks and mortar, whether rented or owned.

Close your eyes and breathe gently. Make the inner request, "Let me see where I have been living." For a few moments, explore the images, scenery, and moods you are shown. Now say, "Let me see my true home." For a few moments, witness the sights that arise. Opening your eyes, resolve to live each day more fully in the atmosphere of your true home, whatever the limitations of the circumstances around you.

·132·

Sometimes, without there being one word spoken between two people, thoughts and feelings are transferred without people knowing it, through the current of breath. Breath is a link with which one individual is connected with another individual; and space does not make a difference if once the connection of the breath is established. The communication will be sure and clear, if only the wire is tied to sympathetic hearts.

Words are vocalized breath. With or without these sound sculptures, breath always sends a message. In reality, the lapping waves of a person's atmosphere speak louder than anything the person could verbalize in language. Breath expresses an energetic transmission by which the soul, heart, and body make a variety of declarations, sometimes conscious but often unconscious.

When interacting with people in the course of the day, pay less attention to their features, clothes, and mannerisms, and more attention to the tone of their breath. Listen to what their breath is telling you. Then try to send a message in reply by means of your own breath. You need not abandon the use of words, but see what happens when you treat words as an accessory rather than as the essential substance of communication.

·133·

As the air, by being caught in the water, becomes a bubble for the moment; and as a wave of the air, being caught in a hollow vessel, becomes a sound; so intelligence, caught by the mind and body, becomes the soul. Therefore, intelligence and soul are not two things; it is only a condition of intelligence that is the soul. Intelligence, in its original aspect, is the essence of life, the spirit of God.

God breathed, and the Great Spirit was God's breath. Where the Great Spirit flows unsounded and unbounded, it's called intelligence. When it enters into conjunction with minds and bodies, it's known as soul. All souls are one in essence; they become many in the unfolding of their diverse pathways of experience. Manyness leads back to oneness—but then, again, the ancient singularity blossoms in multitudinousness.

Close your eyes and let your breath become long, wide, and deep. As you inhale, feel your mind merging into your soul. Watch your thoughts flow into the soul's river of awareness. Now briefly hold your breath, making sure to avoid strain of any kind. While your breath is held, let the river of your soul empty itself in the ocean of pure intelligence. In that ocean there is no distinction between the knower and the known. All is sheer luminous presence. As you exhale, the ocean floods into the river. At the culmination of your exhalation, your soul reaches into your workaday mind.

·134·

When one thinks of the body, it has many organs. When one thinks of the mind, it has various thoughts. When one thinks of the heart, it has many feelings. But when one thinks of the soul in the right sense of the word, it is one single being. It is above division, and therefore it is the soul that really can be called an individual.

The soul is simplicity itself. Its simplicity is its innocence, and its innocence is its light. The soul's light is the light of pure knowing, the radiance of the primordial intelligence kindled by the One Being at the beginning of time, a radiance that will blaze until the end of time, and even beyond it. The body and mind revolve around the soul, both constantly changing. For its part, the soul never changes.

Gaze into a mirror. First, focus on the image of your face. Recognize it as your incarnate persona, your physical avatar. How it is now is not how it has always been or will always be. It is a snapshot of a moment soon to be consigned to the past. Now let your face lose focus and slightly blur. Shift your attention from the object of your glance to your glance itself. However you have looked in the course of your life, and whatever moods and opinions you have entertained, the essence of that glance has always remained the same. It's your soul's act of witnessing. It will assume eyes of a different kind when your eyes of flesh are no more.

·135·

There is a longing hidden beneath all other longings a person has, and that longing is for freedom. This longing is sometimes satisfied by a walk in solitude, in the woods; when one is left alone to be by oneself for a time; when one is fast asleep, and even dreams do not trouble one; and when one is in meditation in which, for the moment, the activities of body and mind both are suspended. Therefore, the sages have preferred solitude and have always shown love for nature. And they have adopted meditation as the method of attaining that goal that is the freedom of the soul.

The soul is simultaneously pulled in two directions: toward the frontier of manifestation in search of joy, and toward the center of its own being in remembrance of its original freedom. When weariness mounts and the hitherto fascinating monde of pleasures and conquests dulls and loses its sheen, the satisfying recourse is always solitude and the company of speechless beings. Finding itself alone, the soul finds itself.

Go on a solitary walk in a place where wildness still has a foothold. Leave behind your hopes and fears. Rather than thinking about the stones, trees, and clouds that surround you, make yourself transparent so that the landscape effortlessly passes through your mind and soul and is absorbed into the infinite. Be nothing more or less than a magnifying glass in the hand of the Seer of All.

·136·

Death, in point of fact, does not belong to the soul; and so it does not belong to the person. Death comes to what the person knows, not to the person. Life lives, death dies. But the mind that has not probed the depth of the secret of life becomes perplexed and unhappy over the idea of death.

Physical structures are constantly corroding and disintegrating. The cells that compose our bodies are replaced year after year, but it won't be long before these bodies we wear will dissolve altogether. The idea of death is a haunting one when the body and the self are assumed to be one and the same. Reality will eventually disabuse the mind of that bleak illusion.

Go for a walk in a cemetery. Read the headstones as you pass them, learning the names of the interred, the years in which they flourished in bodily form, and the relations that existed between some of them. Could the life that burned so brightly in them have disappeared forever? Anticipate your own eventual death. Can the light that brightens your eyes ever truly die? Ask yourself: "What is it in me that is mortal, and what is destined to endure?"

·137·

Intelligence is not only a knowing faculty but is creative at the same time. The whole manifestation is the creation of the intelligence. Time and space both are nothing but the knowledge of the intelligence. The intelligence, confined to this knowledge, becomes limited; but when it becomes free from all knowledge, then it experiences its own essence, its own being.

Intelligence is the essence from which the Creator has created the world and all that it contains. Intelligence finds manifestation first as an abstract consciousness, then as a mind entranced by images, and finally as a physical entity—the form we call the universe. Along the way it yields multitudes, becoming, as it does, the soul of countless souls, the mind of innumerable minds, and the body of myriad bodies. Each of us is a microcosm of that sprawling macrocosm, a miniature exemplar of the timeless archetype that it is.

Close your eyes and breathe with calm vigilance. Attend to your body and its sensations. Conceive it as a fragment of the universal body. As you inhale, draw primal sap from the great body into your frame. Exhaling, situate your physicality in the anatomy of the cosmos. Now attend to your mind and its thoughts. Consider it a fraction of the universal mind. Inhaling, gather fresh funds of sentience from the overmind into your psyche. Exhaling, upload your cognition into the mind of minds. Finally, attend to your soul. Know it to be a facet of the universal soul. As you inhale and exhale, noetic light circulates freely between the part and the whole in constant waves of systole and diastole.

·138·

It is this that the Sufis call the process of unlearning, which purifies, or makes intelligence free from knowledge. It is the glimpses of that experience that is called ecstasy, for then the intelligence has an independent joy that is true happiness.

A sure route to rediscovering the soul's way of knowing is to suspend, temporarily, the mode of knowledge familiar to the body-mind nexus. When a person's second nature freezes in its tracks, something long forgotten steps out of the shadows. It goes against the grain of habit to disregard what seems obvious to the body and mind, even for a moment. But only the empty-headed are shown the vastness of space. Unknowingness towers over every species of acquired cleverness. When the soul has reacquainted itself with its original simplicity it can afford to take up again what the body and mind have learned, now without the price of alienation.

Set out on the path of unlearning. Even while navigating the various encounters of the day and responding rationally to circumstances as you find them, in your heart of hearts keep repeating the thought, "I don't know." Consider nothing to be as it seems, take nothing for granted, and confess to yourself, again and again, that reality is always beyond what can possibly be conceived. Look for existence not in this thing or that, but in the act of looking.

·139·

Once the soul has risen above this illusive phase of life by climbing on the top of all that is besides the soul itself, it experiences, in the end, that happiness for which this whole creation took place. The discovering of the soul is the uncovering of God.

The universe is no accident. It is, instead, a cascading disclosure of its own infinite source and essence. First the One sends out the many to show them its limitless signs in themselves and each other. Then it calls them back to itself, showing them that nothing was ever separate from anything else and that they themselves have no being apart from the one who lives in them, the One itself. Manyness now reappears, but a manyness rendered translucent, whereas it was once opaque. At the heart of it all, the uncreated light perpetually blazes, ceaselessly emanating its inexhaustible compassion. And so the One knows itself in the many and the many come to know themselves in the One.

Pledge yourself to the quest to find God. Take this task more deeply to heart than any other, putting it at the very center of your life. Look for your soul within the soul of souls and find God as its outbreather and inbreather, at once overwhelmingly majestic and intimately familiar.

·140·

The soul, during its journey toward manifestation and during its stay on any plane, whether in the sphere of the angels, of the jinns, or of human beings, feels attraction toward its source and goal. Some souls feel more attraction than others, but there is an unconscious or conscious indrawing felt by every soul.

There is homesickness in every human heart, and no one will find lasting satisfaction until that quiet but raking nostalgia is properly honored. The frantic conditioned mind tries to bury it under a thousand distractions, but it will not stay subdued for long. Better to welcome it and adopt it as one's own. Like a beacon, it leads those who give it its due to the holy garden that is the soul's true abode.

Close your eyes and compose your breath. When a state of relaxation comes over you so that your chest and belly rise and fall with ease, ask yourself, "What do I deeply miss?" Images of departed loved ones might come to your mind, or of bygone days when life was especially sweet. Acknowledge these images with affection, but then look beyond them. Look past all conceivable images and, in the further distance, survey what now emerges, a looming array of diaphanous and vaporous states of being that hover at the boundaries of memory. These states are, in their way, the cumulus, stratus, and cirrus clouds of your native land. Glide down through their mists on a beam of sunlight until your feet touch the ground of your everlasting home.

·141·

Life is interesting in its every phase on the journey toward manifestation, as well as on the soul's return toward the goal. Every moment of life has its peculiar experience, one better than the other, one more valuable than the other. In short, life may be said to be full of interest. Sorrow is interesting, as well as joy. There is a beauty in every phase of life, if only one can learn to appreciate it.

No experience in life is wasted. One day might have been delightful and another dismal, but opposites make for contrast and contrast brings the colors of existence into sharp perspective–otherwise all is gray. It's the villain that creates the hero and the valley that raises the peak. Even the soul's forgetting proves to have had a purpose, seeing how a whole world is quickened by its reawakening, and the floodgates of boundless mercy are swung open as if for the first time. And this, still, is not the end.

Look back on a difficult event in your life. Acknowledge the suffering you experienced as something real and not to be lightly dismissed. At the same time, see how the matter does not end there. The episode is part of a larger picture, and in that expanded tableau a story is unfolding that has a sacred meaning. Every part of the story is sanctified by the meaning of the whole of it. It is a meaning that can never be put into words, and yet it is real—far more real than any part of the tale interpreted in isolation. Sense that indescribable meaning in your very bones.

·142·

What is the return journey? Where does one return? When does one return? The return begins from the time the flower has come to a full bloom. From the moment the plant has touched its summit, from the time the object, the purpose for which a soul is born on earth, is fulfilled; for then there is nothing to hold it, and the soul naturally draws back, like breath drawn in.

Every soul is destined to realize and, in some fashion, bring to flower a personal life, and only then is the soul called back. Some souls find the culmination of their individuality among the angels and proceed no further. Others actualize it among the jinn and duly return. Still others fulfill their vocations in the physical realm. And then there are those who pursue their tenacious devotions into the hereafter, and only there, once more among the jinn or the angels, unfurl at full length the petals of their scarred but beating hearts.

A flower contains a seed fated to enter the earth when the flower falls and crumbles to pieces. The act of blooming unveils the flower's hitherto secret color and fragrance in a bright crescendo of self-giving. It also signals the flower's impending dissolution, when its petals will again become soil. Sense the slow budding of your heart in the ripening of your personal destiny. Feel the hour coming—appointed on a day only God knows—when your heart will reach full flower. Let yourself be ineluctably drawn by that promise, and ready, afterward, to sink as a silent seed into the depths of the earth.

·143·

The connection of the body and the soul is like one's attachment to one's dress. It is one's duty to keep the dress in good order, for one needs it to live in the world; but it is ignorance, a great ignorance indeed, when one forgets oneself and knows oneself as the dress.

To have a thing and not be had by the having of it is a subtle and noble art. Only after a dizzying succession of heartbreaks and breakthroughs in its winding trek through the world does the self at last learn, God willing, to care for things and people without clinging to them—to "kiss the joy as it flies," as the poet said.

The final washing of the body, when its breath has departed, is conceivably the most intimate act that one person can perform toward another. Close your eyes, compose your breath, and calmly imagine your body in its final repose. Visualize benevolent and trusted hands gently laving your limbs. The action honors your body at the same time as it consigns it, finally, to the elements. Within the churning gyres of earth, water, fire, and air your molecules will now be pressed into the anatomies of innumerable things and creatures yet to be born.

·144·

Life and death are both contrary aspects of one thing, and that is change. If there remains anything of death with the soul who has passed away from this earth, it is the impression of death according to the idea it has of death. If the soul had a horror of death, it carries that horror with it. If it had an agitation against death, it carries that impression.

Expectations tend to fulfill themselves. Death takes on the form that a person imagines. Those who fear it as a horrible fate prepare themselves to be terrified. On the other hand, those who anticipate it as a welcome sublimation of the spirit prepare themselves to be transfigured. In the first case, the angel of death appears as a scowling grim reaper, and in the second as an amiable usher.

Contemplate your attitude toward death. Anticipate the moment of your death and ask yourself how you will meet it. Death could come to any of us at any time. Are you ready, at any moment, to walk through the portal between worlds without despair?

·145·

Besides, the dying soul carries with itself the impression of the idea and regard that those surrounding it in life had for death, especially at the time of its passing from the earth. This change, for some time, paralyzes every activity of the soul. The soul that has become impressed by the idea that it held itself of death, and by the impression that was created by its surroundings round the deathbed, is kept in a state of inertia—call it fear, horror, depression, or disappointment.

A person approaching death is helped by the presence of friends and family who radiate love and trust in life's endlessness. Faces wracked with fear and voices choked with sobs cannot give ease or hope to the heart of one about to leap beyond flesh and blood. What the heart needs at that moment is not a harangue against death but an acceptance of its sacred mystery, together with gentle expressions of an affection that will never end.

One cannot always control the nature of one's surroundings, even at the most pivotal moments of one's life. Death might come in a quiet place or in the middle of sheer chaos. One can, however, wrap oneself in the atmosphere one chooses. It's possible to call on holy beings—prophets, saints, and angels—and to experience their presence. It's within one's power to conjure up an oasis imbued with the fragrances of all things acknowledged in one's heart as beautiful. By cultivating this plot of imaginative land day after day, frequenting it in the midst of all kinds of circumstances, one keeps it ready.

·146·

How many souls prove simple in believing the idea of death, and carrying with them the same idea while passing from the earth to a life that is a greater life still? And how many souls will we find in the world who believe the end of life to be death, a belief in mortality that cannot be rooted out from their minds? The whole teaching of Jesus Christ has, as its central theme, to rise toward the realization of immortality.

To suppose oneself extinguished while still burning strong is a strange state in which to find oneself. A person in this condition is not dead, since the soul never dies, but neither is such a person entirely alive. The sufferer of death's illusion vegetates weakly in the hereafter until the realization of life's persistence slowly dawns. Then, at last, it's possible to rise up and go on. By contrast, those acquainted with the meaning of death face no confusion and no delay.

Life changes its form constantly, but is never destroyed. Turn within and let your intuition guide you. Ask yourself, "When my heart stops beating, what in me will end and what will

continue?" Carefully observe what you are shown. At the be-
ginning and end of each day, spend a moment intentionally
occupying the dimension of your being that will survive death.

·147·

So there comes the impulse of life that, breaking through this cloud of mortality, makes the soul see the daylight after the darkness of the night. And what does the soul see in this bright daylight? It sees itself living as before, having the same name and form, and yet progressing. The soul finds a greater freedom in this sphere and less limitation than it had previously experienced in its life on the earth.

Life in the hereafter is not, at first, formless. The body of vision endures even when its physical counterpart is scattered to the winds. As in a dreamscape, the soul wears the name and form it has worn in the world. The story continues where it left off. Old acquaintances are rekindled and new connections are made. And there is now more room in which to move.

Dreams occur mostly in the shadowlands of the world of images. Veridical dreams are the exception—these shimmering visions reveal the imaginative world in its true colors. Dreamers usually forget their dreams in the morning. If you resolve to remember your dreams when going to sleep and then try to recall them as soon as you wake up, you are likely to be shown a glimpse of the events of the night. The more one tries to

remember the more one usually does remember. By familiariz-
ing yourself with your dream body you prepare to live and move
in the body of vision in the hereafter.

·148·

Before the soul now is a world—a world not strange to it, but the world that it has made during its life on the earth. That which the soul has known as mind, that very mind, to the soul, now is a world. That which the soul called, while on earth, imagination, is now before it, a reality. If this world is artistic, it is the art produced by this soul. If there is the absence of beauty, that is also the neglect of the soul toward beauty while on earth.

This is the kingdom that the soul has made while on earth, as a bird builds its nest to stay there during the autumn. This is the autumn of the soul, which is the hereafter. It passes this autumn in the world that it has made either agreeable or disagreeable for itself.

The world we are due to enter through the door of death is by no means an alien world. On the contrary it is a deeply familiar place, because it is the condition of our own mind. It harbors everything we've ever imagined, and its most prominent monuments and landmarks follow the lines of thought that have most often occupied our earthly minds. The hereafter reproduces the measure of loveliness we have gathered into our hearts in this world.

Continually ask yourself, "What do I wish to bring home?"
Recognize that every act of imagination and attention leaves
an imprint on the landscape that will one day be your personal
habitat—and indeed, deep down, already is.

·149·

But one might ask, "Do you mean to say that the soul lives a solitary life in this world it has made?" No, how can it be solitary? This mind, the secret of which so few know in the world, this mind can be as large as the world and larger still. This mind can contain all that exists in the world and even all that the universe contains in itself.

Does one then see all those one has known while on the earth? Yes, especially those whom one has loved most and hated most.

Creation is a palace of mirrors, and everything exists in relation to everything else. To say that we will live in our minds in the hereafter is not to say that we will be alone. Our minds contain the presences of many others, and we have a presence in many minds. Those we love are very present within us. Alas, so too are those who arouse in us ongoing thoughts of hatred–if such people exist. We are fatefully tied to those we habitually think of.

When you hold a grudge, consider the cost. The more you think of a person who has offended you, the closer that person comes to you. Forgetting brings release and relief. How can you forget someone who has acted so abhorrently? By entrusting the whole matter to God's hands and being done with it. The justice and redeeming power of the One can be depended on. Now is the perfect time to move on.

·150·

If one has learned, while on earth, how to create joy and happiness for oneself and for others, in the other world, that joy and happiness will surround one. And if one has sown the seeds of poison while on earth, the fruits one has to reap there, one must reap there.

One gets what one gives. The truth of this proposition may not seem evident in the present world, where greed is often rewarded, but the hereafter will prove it. The world of images is a world not only of justice, but of poetic justice. In that world hymns become doves that return to their senders with leafy sprigs and slanders become foul hazes that cling to their authors until purification is undertaken and forgiveness attained.

When someone wrongs you, it's easy to resent it. What requires more insight is to look deeper. Those who cause others harm essentially harm themselves. Whether there are witnesses or not, that person has taken on a burden of accountability that will have to be reckoned with. If the reckoning doesn't happen here, it will happen in the hereafter. Recognizing this, it's possible to transform one's resentment into genuine compassion for the person who has taken on such an onerous debt.

·151·

Every hour, every moment in life has its judgment. There is no doubt about it, but why, especially, the Judgment Day has been mentioned in the scriptures to take place in the hereafter is because in the hereafter one cover from the soul has been lifted up. Therefore, the judgment that every soul experiences here on earth and yet remains ignorant of, being unconscious of it, becomes more clearly manifest to the view of a soul who has passed from this earth.

In this world, we only see what our eyes show us. We don't see the full effects of our words and actions. Nonetheless, every gesture of our hand sends out ripples. In the hereafter, everything we have done, and its impact, will stand revealed. Every word we have spoken will reecho. There will be no denying any of it. There will be judgment—*and*, we may trust, the presence of the mercy that brought the universe into being at the beginning of time.

Recollect the myriad words you have spoken in the course of your life. Which sentences crafted in your mouth would you be happy to hear repeated to you, and which would now make you cringe? As you look ahead to the years that remain to you, resolve to say only words that you will welcome meeting again.

·152·

What connection has the soul who has passed from the earth with those who are still on the earth? No doubt there is a wall now that divides those on this earth from those on the other plane; yet the connection of the heart still remains intact and unbroken as long as the link of sympathy is there.

If you love someone, your love does not lessen if they travel to the other side of the planet, or if they leave the physical world altogether. Love, as we know, is a cord that is capable of stretching endlessly. So long as that cord is sound, communication is always possible.

Close your eyes and gently lengthen your breath. Turn your attention toward a loved one who is no longer embodied in the physical world. Over the space of a number of breaths, as you exhale send out an earnest greeting, as though reaching out a hand into the invisible. Then shift your focus to your inhalation and listen. The answer may not come in words. But listen with rapt attention, and attend to what reaches you from the invisible.

·153·

What does a soul do after having arrived at the sphere of the jinn? It continues to do the same that it has been doing, right or wrong, good or bad. It goes along the same lines that it has gone through life. Is there no progress for that soul? Yes, there is, but in the same direction. No ultimate change necessarily takes place. Yes, the soul finds itself in more clear spheres and therefore knows its way better than it had known before, when on earth.

Potters will keep spinning pots in the next world, and gardeners will go on planting seeds and pruning hedges. The glaze on the pots will gleam with a luster not seen before, and the roses will exude an otherworldly aroma. Thieves will keep stealing until the stark transparency of their crimes, together with the glaring consequences for all concerned, makes continuing unpalatable.

Which art, science, or craft has, since long years, riveted your attention and given you occasion to hone your skill? That which all vocational paths have in common is that they extend beyond the visible horizon, and there is always more to discover and create. Close your eyes and compose your breath.

Think of your lifework. Imagine it not merely fading out, but instead undergoing an eloquent renewal in the world beyond. Sense the further fulfillment that is possible, and let yourself be guided toward it in all that you do with care while still in this world.

·154·

What is its destination? The same destination may be hidden under a thousand objects; every soul is bound for the same goal. How can it be otherwise? Fancy how one becomes attached to a place where one has been before, how one is attracted to a spot in the solitude where once one sat and enjoyed the beauty of nature. How much then the soul must be attracted, either consciously or unconsciously, to its source, which is its eternal abode.

People pursue diverse callings, but what everyone seeks is beauty. One person tracks it in elegant lines while another hunts after it in undulating notes. Some pursue its secret through the exercise of power; others take the route of self-giving. Each seeker's quest leads deeper into the mystery of beauty, and beauty is never exhausted. Beauty of form culminates in formless beauty, and in that vastness all paths converge in a homeland without end.

Close your eyes and gradually refine your breath. As your breath becomes a rhythmic and pellucid swing, let it carry your thought into ever deeper layers of meaningfulness. Contemplate the experience of beauty–not the form of a particular thing of beauty, but the sensation of beholding what is beautiful, in whatever form. What all forms of beauty have in common is a consanguinity of spirit that bespeaks their shared origin in the home of the witness's soul.

·155·

Is there no wall between the people on the earth and those who have passed away from this earth? Yes, there is a wall, which only stands before those who are still on the earth, but not before the ones who have passed on to the other side.

What do they do in order to experience life in the physical world? They seek for an accommodation in the heart of a being on the earth and focus themselves on the mind of the person, and receive, through this medium, all the knowledge and experience of this earth as clearly as this person.

Just as humans see the ants that crawl beneath them more distinctly than ants see the humans that tramp above them, those who have left this world are able to perceive those still within it more clearly than the reverse. But it isn't exactly that the people of that world beyond peer down from above. Instead, by means of an act of empathic seeing that comes naturally to the denizens of the jinnic world, they look out through the eyes of those on whom they choose to concentrate their minds.

The empathic seeing that is possible in the next world is foreshadowed in this world. Think of someone who is dear to your heart. Close your eyes and imagine stepping into their shoes.

Put aside your own characteristics and immerse yourself entirely in the vantage point of the person you are concentrating on. Vividly imagine how it would be to inhabit their form, walk with their gait, speak with their voice, and see the world through their eyes. After a few moments, return to your own perspective and open your eyes.

·156·

Are there any spirits who care little for the life they have left behind? Many, among them good ones who are only concerned with the journey onward. It is those, as a rule, whose heart, so to speak, is still attached to the life of the earth and in whose heart the interest for the journey onward has not yet been kindled; it is they who are inclined to keep in communication with this world.

There are exceptions; there are spirits who, out of kindness to a few or to many, wish to still keep in connection with the earth in order to serve and to be useful. But the spirits of the latter kind still go on advancing toward the goal, instead of detaining themselves in communicating with the people on the earth.

In the hereafter, most souls accept the onward march of life and content themselves with the reality of the present and the promise of the future. There are some, however, who cannot let go of the past. They turn back to the places they knew in the world, and linger there indefinitely. They are known as ghosts. There are others who turn back to the physical world repeatedly, but for another reason. Their motive is to be of service. They are called bodhisattvas.

The great beings of the past are remembered for the uplifting legacies they have left behind. You might find, at certain points in your life, that you come under the wing of one of them. The saint or sage becomes a guardian or guiding spirit whose presence you sometimes feel—not as a concept pertaining to the past, but as an immediate intuition in the present moment, as real as the presence of someone in the room. By inwardly attuning to the figure, you prepare yourself for these contacts.

·157·

The soul is the divine breath; it purifies, revivifies and heals the instrument in which it functions. On its return journey the soul shows the same phenomenon in a different way. From all the impressions of illness, of sadness, of miseries that the soul had experienced while on the earth and had taken into the spirit world, it heals its being and renews the tissues of that body that still remains with it after having left the physical body. It purifies it from all illness and its impressions, and thus renews its life in the spirit world in accordance to its evolution.

The breath of the Infinite blows through the soul. Wherever the soul spreads its influence, life flourishes. When the soul is eclipsed, leaves shrivel and cracks cleave the earth. Every unveiling of the soul is a healing and a resurrection. Since the soul lies at the core of all beings, in the end no one will be denied its balm.

When in the grip of pain or anxiety, go to a place free of clutter and noise. Feel your feet rooted in the ground and your crown open to the sky. Draw the pure essence of the air that swirls around you into your lungs, into your blood, and into the depths of your heart. Let yourself be drawn to the center of your existence. Avoid imposing a preconception on the mysterious power you touch there; simply contact it, and receive what it has for you in the moment.

·158·

The soul is on a continual journey. In whatever plane, it is journeying all the time; and in this journey it has a purpose to accomplish, many purposes contained and hidden in one purpose. There are objectives that remain unfulfilled in one's lifetime on the earth. They are accomplished in the further journey in the spirit world, for nothing that the human heart has once desired remains unfulfilled.

The soul travels in the sense that it projects itself through a succession of minds, the first preincarnate, the second embodied, and the third resurrected. In each transition, something is lost and something else is gained. At the same time, much is conserved from state to state. Possibilities conceived before birth are pursued in the world, and desires unfulfilled in the world are realized after death.

Close your eyes, enter into a state of lucid calm, and turn your attention to the center of your chest. Ask yourself, "What do I desire?" Let the question pass over you in continuous waves, each wave drawing you deeper into the nature of your heart's yearning. Keep the executive function of your psyche well in the background; this isn't the time to draw up plans or evaluate pros and cons. Simply meet your heart's sincerest wish and know it.

·159·

In the soul's coming on earth and its return, in both there is a process to be seen. When coming on earth, it adorns itself with the covers of the particular planes through which it passes; and on its return, it uncovers itself from the bodies it has adopted for the convenience of experiencing that particular plane. In this way, it is a process of covering and uncovering.

Mollusks forge shells out of gleanings from seawater, shells that are at last pounded into sand. Similarly, our physical carapaces equip us to live for a time in the ocean of matter, but must eventually be returned to its vortex of transmutation. The same is true of our minds, whose substance will likewise be reclaimed, though after a longer duration.

Close your eyes. Visualize the moment when your mind will relinquish your body, leaving it to merge into the anatomies of innumerable bodies, organic and inorganic. Envision the state of existence that will follow. Then imagine the moment when your soul will withdraw from your mind, causing it to disperse into the universal mind. What will be the state of your soul then?

·160·

The condition of the next world is most like the condition of the dream world. In the dream one does not see oneself much different from the way one appears, except in some cases and at some times, and for that there are reasons. Nevertheless, the power that the soul has in the next world is much greater than it has in this world of limitations. The soul in the other world, so to speak, matures and finds within itself the power of which it was ignorant through life: the power of creating and producing all it wishes through life.

In the physical world a person's appearance is largely determined by their ancestry. Of course, disposition and way of life also leave their mark. In the hereafter, the earthly form persists. It is, after all, what the mind knows. But a person's form is more malleable there than here. The body of the world of images is as one confidently imagines it.

Close your eyes and still your mind. Think of someone you know. First, visualize the person prosaically, which is to say, exactly as they appear in daily life. Then visualize the person poetically; in other words, as their spirit reveals itself to you in its fullness, albeit still in visible form. Now turn your mind's gaze toward yourself. Envision your body first as it appears in the mirror, and second as it will appear when remolded "nearer to the heart's desire."

·161·

The soul, on its way toward the goal in the spheres of jinn, has some riches collected during its life on the earth in the form of merits, qualities, experience and convictions, talents, attitude, and a certain outlook on life. In spite of the belongings of the earth that it has returned to the earth on its passing, this soul in the spirit world offers these riches, allows them to be taken from it, and imparts them to the souls coming from their source who are on their way to the earth.

In the hereafter, émigrés from the physical world will find that their terrestrial learnings and acquirements are of special interest to newly descending souls. The transfer of knowledge between souls traveling in opposite directions is a kind of re-incarnation. The departed soul does not return to the physical world, but some of the soul's aptitudes may indeed return, carried now by another soul.

Consider the most important channels of your psyche. You might find that some of these proctivities derive from the various experiences in your life, while others are traceable to the legacies of your parents and ancestors. The question arises, do these sources account for all of your inclination and talents, or is there an element in you that neither nature nor nurture can explain? If there is, can you intuit—in the manner, almost, of a myth—a basis, an initiation, preceding your life on earth?

·162·

Does the spirit impart its merits, talents, experience, and knowledge to the new-coming soul passing through the spirit plane to the earth, consciously or unconsciously? Sometimes it imparts this consciously, in some cases unconsciously; but in the conscious action there is the greatest pleasure for the spirit. For this soul, which is taking the knowledge from a spirit as its heritage from the world of the jinn, is considered by the spirit as a child by its parents or a pupil by the teacher. In the heritage of this soul there is a great joy for that spirit.

Just as an author is able to reach into the imaginations of multitudinous readers without ever meeting them, the streams of emanation that flow between disembodied minds do not always involve mutual acquaintance. But when the giver of a spiritual bequest knows and esteems the one to whom it is given, the bestowal carries a particular meaningfulness.

Our minds have collected a great deal of clutter. On reflection, only a fraction of our accumulated freight is likely to prove worthy of preserving, let alone passing on to someone else—and particularly to a pure soul freshly arrived from the

*innermost spheres of existence. And yet every life has its har-
vest, every beating heart its distilled elixir. Ask yourself, "What
is the yield of my life that I would readily pass on to another
soul if something of the kind were to be asked of me?"*

·163·

A soul lives in the spirit world while it is busy accomplishing the purpose of its life, which may last for thousands of years. Does a soul in the spirit world continue to do the same work that it did during its life on the earth? Yes, it does in the beginning, but it is not bound to the same work for this reason: that it is not subject to limitations as it was while on the earth. The soul eventually rises to that standard that was the standard of its ideal. It does that work that was its desire.

A large part of the work of our world consists of effort expended with the sole motive of earning one's bread. For the fortunate, work is an opportunity to explore a passion, develop a skill, or contribute to the welfare of others. For many exhausted toilers in fields and factories, however, work is drudgery, a necessary evil pursued for no other reason than to keep soul and body together.

In the hereafter, all work will be meaningful. Work will be the means by which souls realize their life's purpose. Most will initially continue the work that they did in the world. Some will discover deeper levels of significance and possibility in the professions they had pursued before death. Others will advance to other fields, and will find their fulfillment there. Attainments and creations only vaguely groped toward here will find their crystalline realization there. Along the way, the incandescence of every burgeoning life work will irradiate and quicken untold others.

Think of your vocation as a sprawling territory. Behind you lie the attainments you have already achieved. Before you stand the challenges you must now face. Look into the far distance, where land meets sky. What magnifications, refinements, and integrations beckon you from the distant horizon, destined to be realized at last, whether in this world or the next?

·164·

The spirit world is incomprehensible to the mind, which is only acquainted with the laws of the physical world. An individual who is a limited being here, is as a world there. A soul is a person here and a planet there. When one considers the helplessness of this plane, one cannot for a single moment imagine the facility, the convenience, the comfort as the possibilities of the next world.

Certain laws hold true there as well as here. There, like here, nothing exists in isolation; everything is sustained through a pulsing web of reciprocal relations. But there are also striking differences between the two worlds. On the physical plane, entropy is a constant hindrance. In the world beyond, friction is minimal, and emergent synergies are dazzlingly prolific.

Early in life, children are generally given to understand by their elders that their imaginative visions are impractical whims that should be once and for all put aside in favor of the sober prag-matism that a competitive world demands. Thus do dreams die. Ask yourself, "Is there a hallowed vision I have long hidden, or half forgotten, in the face of the world's apathy?" If you find that you do, indeed, harbor a secret of this kind, contemplate the picture of its fulfillment, whether in this world or the next.

·165·

Life in the spheres of the jinns is the phenomenon of mind. The mind is not the same there, with all the thoughts and imaginations that it carries from the earth to this plane. Mind is a mind here, and the whole being there. Thoughts are imaginations here, but reality there. One thinks here, but the same action there, instead of a thought, becomes a deed. For action, which here depends upon the physical body, there becomes the act of the mind.

Here in the material world we are known only by the words we speak and the actions we perform. Unless they are expressed in a tangible form, thoughts are considered purely personal and inconsequential. Words and deeds, however, always have their roots in thought. In truth, thought forms are just as real as physical things and actions—in a sense, they are more real— only they occupy another zone of reality, a region rationalism dismisses as subjective. The consequentiality of thought and imagination will become perfectly clear when our minds live wholly within themselves.

When you think of a thing, do you discover it or create it in the world of images? Both are true. Everything conceivable already exists there in potential, but whatever is thought is actualized, and progressively intensified with the deepening and protraction of the thought. Reflect on the thoughts you find yourself returning to day after day. Do you find that your priorities are in proper order: Are the thoughts you most often take up the ones to which you most truly wish to give life? If not, it's never too late to pivot.

·166·

The pessimists stand against their own light and mar their own object here, and more so in the hereafter, where desire is the seed that is sown on the soil of the spirit world. And optimism is the water that rears the plant. But knowledge at the same time gives that sunshine that helps the plants to flourish on the earth as well as in the spheres of the jinns.

In this world, pessimists and naysayers frequently miss important chances. In the hereafter the loss will be even greater, because faith and imagination are the two wings that enable the soul to fly. Fortunately there are second chances, and even the most stubborn cynic will eventually learn to see signs and wonders.

Close your eyes, slowly lengthen your breath, and turn within. Look into the depths of yourself and find there a sincere aspiration toward a sublime possibility. Is the light of the wish clear and bright, or is it dimmed by shadows? If there are shadows, inquire into their nature. What are the doubts and fears they embody? If there are special considerations to contend with, acknowledge them. But rather than letting these reservations obscure the light of your wish, take the light as your guide, and trust that all complications will be resolved as you proceed step-by-step.

·167·

Is there a death for the spirits in the spheres of the jinns? Yes, they have it, but after a much longer time; a death not so severe as on the earthly plane.

What especially brings about death in the sphere of the jinns is the moment when hope gives way and there is no more ambition there. It is the loss of enthusiasm that is a death there and the cause of death here on the earth. When it loses the strength and magnetism that hold the soul functioning in it, it falls like a star from heaven, and the soul departs to its own origin.

Death is an act of renunciation. When the soul gives up the body, the life of the hereafter commences. Many interests and preoccupations carry over, however, from one world to the next. In the world of images, the passions and projects of the physical world are brought to fruition. At last, when the mind is sated and the body of visions wearied, the soul renounces jinndom and flies to the angelic world.

Notice how your involvement with situations, people, places, and things lasts as long as your interest and enthusiasm lasts. When your attention wanes, change soon follows. To flit from place to place without fidelity or fruit is to lead a superficial existence. On the other hand, to become rigidly attached to a fixed set of circumstances is to stagnate and languish. For everything there is a time. Consider the course of your life and the station in which you now find yourself. What features of your life are you ready to gracefully renounce? Conversely, where is a greater investment of time and care now needed?

·168·

The soul enters the angelic heavens, and it is allowed to enter the heavens with the same condition as before: it has to leave all that belonged to the sphere of the jinns in that sphere. Thus, by uncovering itself from the garb of the spirit world, it finds its entrance into the world of the angels. Does it take anything from the world of the angels? Yes, not thoughts, but feelings that it may collect. The life of the soul therefore, in this sphere, is felt more by its vibrations.

Thoughts and images are absent from the angelic realm. When angels wear forms, they are wearing apparel assumed in the world of images. In their native land, angels have no shape. Their form is pure light, innocent of contours. For this reason, the geometries and anatomies of the jinnic world cannot be imported to the heaven of lights, though the emotional resonances of physical and imaginative forms do gain admission.

Close your eyes and give your attention to your breath. For a number of moments, identify with your physical body and all that it entails. Acknowledge the self that has its place here. Then withdraw from your senses, sublimate your physical self, and transpose its image to the plane of imagination. For a few moments, linger in an imaginative body. Then disengage from every kind of thought and visualization, essentialize your imaginative identity, and reconstitute your being in the realm of formlessness as a simple light. After a time, retrace your steps and return to the material world.

·169·

The soul in the heaven of the angels, has not got sins or virtues to show; nor has it a heaven or hell to experience, neither does it show any particular ambition or desire. It is either in tune or out of tune. If it is in tune, it takes its place in the music of the heavens as a note in tune. If it is not in tune, it falls short of it, producing a dissonant effect for itself and for others.

In its essence, life is music. Beyond right and wrong, beyond success and failure, there is simply the melody that began when God's breath first brought the universe into being. On the surface, beings have faces. Deep down, we are all particles of song. The task of each being is to sound its note and harmonize with every other note.

Contemplate the world around you as a symphony. Discern its melodic lines and tonal leaps, its crescendos and diminuendos, its surges in complexity and digressions into dissonance. How would the course of your life unfold if you were to adopt the logic of music as your guiding principle?

·170·

What occupation has the soul there? Its occupation is to be around the light and life, like the bee around the flower. What is its sustenance? Its sustenance is divine light and divine life. Divine beauty it sees, divine air it breathes, in the sphere of freedom it dwells, and the presence of God it enjoys.

The angels whirl around the luminous core of being, staggered by prismatic effusions of primal beauty and majesty, reeling in ecstasy, and resounding in wordless hosannas of glorification. Pure light is their air, pure life is their drink, and pure love is their food.

Go on a walk in a park or in a wild place. Leave all of your troubles behind, and let yourself be drawn into a world of splendor. Consider it the first day of creation, since creation is continuously renewed. Regard everything you see as the light of the Face of God. Give yourself over to wonder and awe at the sheer fact of being alive and face-to-face with what is.

·171·

Fancy the music of the heavens, where harmony is in its fullness. What happiness that could give, humans on earth cannot imagine. If the experience of that music is known to anyone, it is to the wakened soul whose body is here, whose heart is in the spheres of the jinns and whose soul is in the heavens of the angels, who while sitting on the earth can experience all the planes of existence.

There are two kinds of happiness, one accidental and the other essential. Accidental happiness is the contentment that comes from favorable circumstances. When all is going well, a person tends to be happy, but when the tide turns, unhappiness sets in. Essential happiness, on the other hand, has no external cause. It's the simple joy that resides in existence itself. This is the emotion of the angels, whose beings are mellifluous in their very essence.

When the conditions around you are favorable, try adopting the inner posture of ignoring the various advantages you are enjoying, and look instead for a happiness that has nothing to do with them. In the same way, when circumstances are unfavorable, give them little heed and seek to unearth the bliss that is innate and constant.

·172·

What body has the soul in the heavens of the angels? Though the soul continues in the spheres of the jinn, with the body in the likeness of the one it had before while on earth, an enormous change takes place in its body and form while in the spheres of the jinn. By the time it departs from there, there is hardly any trace left of the body it had in the spheres of the jinn and before, for it is turned into a luminous being. Its body is then one of radiance, light itself. It may be called intelligence itself.

Just as the physical body ages through the course of life, the jinnic body too gradually transforms. Its lineaments are slowly refined, subtilized, and rendered translucent, so that in the end the pleroma of celestial lights is only a blink away.

Go out in the sunlight, close your eyes, and absorb the warmth of the sun's rays as they stream into your closed eyes and permeate your clothes and the bulk of your body right down to your bones. Sense your anatomy responding with a light of its own. Then take a further step, and observe how the substance of your consciousness is light, a self-luminous light that knows by glowing and glows by knowing.

·173·

The life of the souls in the angelic spheres is incomparably longer than the life of those on the spheres of the jinn. No more desires, no more ambitions, no more strivings have they; only the aspiration to reach further, to experience a greater happiness, a tendency to go on further, closer to that light that is now within their sight. They are flying around this light like the moth around the lantern. The magic lantern, which is the seeking of all souls, is now within their horizon. Nothing else has a greater attraction for them than this light that is continually burning before them.

Life's journey culminates in a vast expanse, almost a timeless one. Everything incidental dissipates. What remains is a deathless allegiance to the essence of reality, a ceaselessly deepening constancy unfolding in waves of bedazzlement, surrender, and rapturous worship. Each sigh draws the soul closer to the Mystery of Mysteries whose being is the consummation of all that exists.

Call a conference of your body, mind, and soul. When all three are present, first address your body and ask, "What is your wish?" Listen to your body's answer and spend a few minutes considering it, without judgment. Next, ask the same question to your mind, and again carefully consider the answer you receive. Thirdly, ask the soul. When your soul tells you the object of its desire, lose yourself in the attraction of what the soul longs for. Finally, recall the wishes of your body and mind, and discern how the soul's desire is reflected in them in a certain fashion.

·174·

The body brought from the angelic heavens covers both the bodies of the sphere of the jinns, as well as of the physical plane, and yet enters into the innermost part of one's being. In this way, the angelic and the jinn bodies not only surround the physical body, but exist within it. When the soul is on its way to the physical plane, its bodies grow and develop and become more distinct; and as the soul advances toward the goal, its bodies become more ethereal and luminous, but indistinct.

When the physical body dies, only its perfume remains in the imaginal body. When the imaginal body dies, what remains is the perfume of the perfume. In the noetic world, the soul is reduced to its essence—an essence that is, however, now subtly engoldened by the cumulative effect of its successive coagulations and dissolutions.

Close your eyes and watch your breath. As you exhale, let your breath reach farther and farther into the distance. As you inhale, concentrate it in your body once again. Exhaling, become progressively empty and transparent, so that at the culmination of your exhalation you are placeless and traceless. Inhaling, shrink and harden into the form of your physical self. For a number of breaths, rhythmically shift back and forth.

·175·

Have they anything to offer to the souls going toward manifestation? Yes, their feelings. In what way do they offer them? The souls coming from the source and going toward the earth are tuned by them, are set to a certain rhythm. It is this offering that determines the line they tread in the future. The Sufis call that day of tuning *ruz-i azal*, the day when the plan was designed for the life of that particular soul.

When a newly manifested soul stands before its creator pledging its eternal fealty, there are witnesses. These witnesses are souls who have descended into time and space and returned. They give their blessings to the one about to embark, and foresee its destiny.

Close your eyes and enter into stillness. Draw up from the well of time the memory of the first moment of your existence, when you stood face-to-face with the one to whom you and all beings belong. Can you recover a trace of the indescribable emotion of that primal moment, the beginning of all that you have seen and known and become?

·176·

There is almost too much that a soul has to do on the earth. There is also much the soul has to accomplish in the spirit world, but there is much less to accomplish in the heavens of the angels. For as the soul proceeds forward, so its burden becomes lighter. The only condition of proceeding forward and drawing closer to the goal is by throwing away the heavy burden that the soul has taken upon itself through its journey.

In the physical world the necessity of food, clothing, shelter, and medicine entails constant exertion. The urge to create is also a powerful motivation, and it becomes stronger still in the hereafter, where the struggle to make ends meet is not so pressing. When the soul reaches the angelic realm, neither survival nor accomplishment command its attention. The soul is at last able to cease becoming, and simply be.

Reflect on the balance of activity and repose in your life. Notice how efforts of various kinds tend to go awry when unbalanced by the ease and renewal that repose brings. Inactivity, however, is not always true rest. Even when the body stops moving, the mind tends to remain in motion—in fact, the mind's flutterings and heavings often increase when a person's hands are unoccupied.

Look for opportunities in the day to enter into complete stillness, a stillness of both body and mind. Whenever you can find a few free moments, spend them doing nothing at all, not thinking about anything, merely existing.

·177·

If one might say that the soul lives thousands of years in the sphere of the jinns, it is millions of years that one can say, for the convenience of expression, that the soul passes in the heavens of angels, until there comes the moment when the soul is most willing to depart even from that plane of love, harmony, and beauty in order to embrace the source and goal of love, harmony, and beauty that has attracted the soul through all planes.

For the soul that has returned to the angelic spheres, the draw of the One is constant and ineluctable. Like a tide that carries a swimmer out to sea, the force of its attraction never slackens. The swimming soul glides through the inner bodies of the galaxies, pulled by an inevitability of infinite fascination and promise.

Close your eyes and enter the inner space of your heart. Silently say the words, "the Perfection of Love." Give your attention to what you are shown. After a few minutes, say the words, "the Perfection of Harmony." Again closely observe what is evoked. Finally say, "the Perfection of Beauty," and witness the meaning that transpires.

·178·

And as the soul has approached nearer, so much closer it has been drawn. It is the unveiling of that radiant garment, which is the body of the soul in the angelic heaven, that brings it to its real destination, the goal that it has continually sought, either consciously or unconsciously. Verily, "From God every soul comes, and to God is its return."

The soul doesn't clutch a guidebook as it nears the Hidden Treasure. Its very body is inscribed with the directions that lead to its long-sought goal. The soul's formless form, it discovers, is nothing less than a map leading home. Its human and jinnic bodies were pages in the same atlas.

Contemplate the meaning of seeking. What have you sought in the course of your life? What has differentiated the objects of your search, and what have they had in common? In what ways has your quest transformed? Can you imagine your search reaching as far as limitlessness? What–or who–is the sought; and who–or what–is the seeker?

·179·

What is this journey, taken by the soul from the source to the manifestation, and from manifestation again to the same source, which is its goal? Is it a journey or is it not a journey? It is a journey in fact and not a journey in truth. It is the change of experiences that makes it a story, and yet the whole story, produced as a moving picture, is on one film that does not travel for miles and miles as it is seen on the screen. Is it many who journey, or one? It is many while still in illusion, and it is one when the spirit has disillusioned itself. Who journeys, is it the human being or God? Both and yet one—two ends of one line.

In one state of being, beings appear, interact, and disappear on the stage of manifestation. In another state, the beings of all times and places exist simultaneously within the vast being who is the body of all bodies, the mind of all minds, and the soul of all souls. In yet another state there is no self or other, no here or there, no body, mind, or soul—and yet the pure essence of life is present: God stands unveiled.

Think of someone you sincerely love. Recall the various occasions when your lives have intersected. In one sense, you are connected to the extent that you have been, and perhaps still remain, in communication. One day, however, earthly communication will end. Will this end the bond between you? Consider how there is a deeper sense in which your link transcends place and time. Your meeting in the world was no accident; it was natural and necessary, since you are allied by destiny. You will certainly meet again in the world beyond. Now take a further step, look into the very heart of the matter, and see how ultimately you are not two different persons. In all of existence, there is only one reality. With the One's exhalation, innumerable beings take shape. With the One's inhalation, everything returns to unity.

·180·

Neither on the earth plane were people their own selves, nor in the sphere of jinns, nor in the heavens of the angels. They were only a captive of their own illusion, caught in a frame, and yet they were not inside it. It was only their reflection. But they saw themselves nowhere, so they could only identify themselves with their various reflections until they realize now that, "I was what I am, and I will be what I was. It was I who was, if there were any; and it is I who will be, if there will be any. It is I who am the source, the traveler, and the goal of this whole existence."

Without departure there can be no homecoming. By leaving home and returning, the traveler comes to know what home is. The journey contains many pains and many joys. In the end, pain and joy become indistinguishable. What remains is the soul's sheer aliveness to life.

Through the vehicle of the soul, the One returns to itself. Each return is the birth and death of a universe and the unveiling of the totality. Love's perfect consummation is its yield.

The returnings continue endlessly.

Wherever you are, whatever you see, whatever you hear, meet the One meeting itself in yearning and wonderment, and lift up a silent hymn of praise.

Verily, truth is all the religion there is, and it is truth that will save.

Amen.

Table of Cross-References

Note: The following table provides cross-references for the boldfaced passages in this book to their location in both *The Soul Whence and Whither* in volume 1 of *The Sufi Message of Hazrat Inayat Khan, Centennial Edition* (New Lebanon, NY: Sulūk Press, 2016) and *The Soul's Journey* (New Lebanon, NY: Omega Publications, 2003).

Immortality	*CE* section/page#	*Soul's Journey* section/page#
1–5	intro/127	intro/3
6	intro/128	intro/3
7	intro/128	intro/4
8	intro/128	intro/4
9	1/132	1/11
10	1/132–33	1/12
11	1/133–34	1/12–13
12	2/138	2/17
13	2/138	2/17
14	2/138	2/17
15	2/138–39	2/17
16	2/139	2/18
17	2/139	2/18
18	3/144	3/23
19	3/144	3/23
20	3/144	3/23
21	3/144–45	3/23
22	3/145	3/24
23	4/149	4/29
24	4/149	4/29

Immortality	*CE* section/page#	*Soul's Journey* section/page#
25	4/149–50	4/29–30
26	4/150	4/30
27	4/150	4/30
28	4/150–51	4/30
29	4/151	4/31
30	6/159	6/39
31	6/159–60	6/39
32	6/160	6/40
33	6/161	6/41
34	7/164	7/45
35	7/165	7/45–46
36	8/170	8/51
37	8/171–72	8/52
38	9/176	9/57
39	9/176	9/57
40	9/177	9/58
41	10/181	10/63
42	10/182	10/64
43	10/182	10/64
44	10/182	10/64
45	10/182	10/64
46	12/190	12/72
47	12/190–91	12/72–73
48	12/191	12/73
49	12/191	12/73
50	12/192	12/74
51	13/195	13/77
52	13/195	13/77

Immortality	*CE* section/page#	*Soul's Journey* section/page#
53	13/196	13/78
54	13/196	13/78
55	13/196	13/78
56	15/207	15/91
57	15/207–8	15/91–92
58	15/208	15/92
59	16/212	16/95
60	16/212	16/95
61	16/212–13	16/95–96
62	16/213	16/96
63	17/218	17/101
64	17/218	17/101
65	17/218–19	17/101
66	17/219	17/102
67	17/219	17/102
68	17/219	17/102
69	17/219–20	17/102–3
70	18/225	18/109
71	18/225	18/109
72	18/225–26	18/109–10
73	18/226	18/110
74	19/229	19/113
75	19/229	19/113
76	19/230	19/114
77	20/233	20/117
78	20/233	20/117
79	20/233	20/117
80	20/233–34	20/117–18

Immortality	*CE* section/page#	*Soul's Journey* section/page#
81	20/234	20/118
82	20/234	20/118
83	20/234–35	20/118–19
84	20/236	20/119–20
85	21/237	21/121
86	21/237–38	21/121–22
87	21/238	21/122
88	21/238	21/122
89	21/238–39	21/122–23
90	23/249	23/133
91	23/249	23/133
92	23/249	23/133
93	23/249–50	23/133–34
94	23/250	23/134
95	24/253	24/137
96	24/253	24/137
97	24/254	24/137–38
98	24/254	24/138
99	25/259–60	25/143
100	25/260	25/143–44
101	25/260	25/144
102	25/260–61	25/144
103	25/261	25/144–45
104	26/263	26/147
105	26/264	26/148
106	27/266	26/151
107	27/266	26/151
108	27/266–67	26/151–52

Immortality	*CE* section/page#	*Soul's Journey* section/page#
109	27/267	26/152
110	27/267	26/152
111	27/267	26/152
112	28/271	28/157
113	28/271	28/157
114	28/272	28/158
115	29/273	29/159
116	29/274	29/15–60
117	29/274	29/160
118	30/277	30/163
119	30/277	30/163
120	30/277–78	30/163–64
121	30/278	30/164
122	31/281	31/167
123	31/283	31/168–69
124	31/283	31/169
125	31/283	31/169
126	32/284	32/171
127	32/284	32/171
128	32/284–85	32/171–72
129	32/285	32/172
130	32/285	32/172
131	32/285	32/172
132	33/290	33/177
133	34/293	34/181
134	34/293–94	34/181–82
135	34/295	34/182–83
136	35/297	35/185

Immortality	CE section/page#	Soul's Journey section/page#
137	35/297	35/185
138	35/297	35/185
139	35/298	35/186
140	36/300	36/191
141	36/300	36/191
142	36/301	36/192
143	36/301	36/192
144	37/306	37/197
145	37/306	37/197
146	37/307	37/198
147	38/313	38/205
148	38/313–14	38/205
149	38/314	38/206
150	38/314	38/206
151	38/314–15	38/206-7
152	38/315	38/207
153	39/318	39/211
154	39/318	39/211
155	39/318–19	39/211–12
156	39/319	39/212
157	40/324	40/217
158	40/324–25	40/217
159	41/329	41/223
160	41/330	41/224
161	43/338	43/233
162	44/343	44/239
163	44/343	44/239
164	44/344	44/240

Immortality	CE section/page#	Soul's Journey section/page#
165	45/349	45/245
166	45/350	45/246
167	45/350	45/246
168	46/355	46/251
169	46/355-56	46/251
170	46/356	46/251-52
171	46/356-57	46/252
172	47/359	47/255
173	47/359-60	47/255
174	47/360	47/256
175	47/360	47/256
176	47/361	47/257
177	47/361	47/257
178	47/361	47/257
179	conc./365	conc./263
180	conc./367	conc./264-65

Inayatiyya

A Sufi Path of Spiritual Liberty

Sulūk Press is an independent publisher dedicated to issuing works of spirituality and cultural moment, with a focus on Sufism, in particular, the works of Hazrat Inayat Khan and his successors. To learn more about Inayatiyya Sufism, please visit **inayatiyya.org**.